CONTENTS

soups & snacks	4
vegetarian	18
seafood	30
poultry	42
meat	54
relishes	86
rice & bread	90
sweets & drinks	104
basics & stocks	114
glossary	116
index	118
facts & figures	119

SOUPS & SNACKS

vegetable pakoras

1. Combine all yogurt mint dipping sauce ingredients in small bowl; cover, refrigerate 1 hour.
2. Sift both flours, spices and salt into a medium bowl. Add garlic; whisk in enough water to make a thick batter. Cover; refrigerate 30 minutes.
3. Boil, steam or microwave cauliflower and broccoli, separately, until just tender; refresh under cold water, drain on absorbent paper.
4. Heat oil in large saucepan. Dip vegetable pieces, one at a time, into batter, drain away excess batter; deep-fry until browned lightly and crisp. Drain on absorbent paper. Repeat process with remaining vegetables. Serve with yogurt mint dipping sauce.

serves 4 to 6

¾ cup (100g) besan (chickpea flour)
¼ cup (35g) self-raising flour
2 teaspoons ground cumin
1 teaspoon garam masala
¼ teaspoon ground turmeric
½ teaspoon chilli powder
2 teaspoons salt
2 cloves garlic, crushed
¾ cup (180ml) water, approximately
1 cup (100g) cauliflower florets
1 cup (85g) broccoli florets
vegetable oil, for deep-frying
1 small eggplant (230g), sliced
2 medium zucchini (240g), sliced

YOGURT MINT DIPPING SAUCE
2 tablespoons bottled mint jelly
¾ cup (180ml) yogurt
1 small red chilli, finely chopped

Whisk water into dry ingredients to make a thick batter.

Drain cooked cauliflower and broccoli on absorbent paper.

Deep-fry battered vegetables until browned lightly and crisp.

bombay mix

1. Heat vegetable oil in large saucepan. Cook pappadums, one at a time, until puffed and crisp; drain on absorbent paper. Cool, break into small pieces.
2. Add rice flakes to same pan; cook, stirring, until flakes are browned lightly. Remove from oil with slotted spoon; drain on absorbent paper. Cool.
3. Combine all spice mixture ingredients in small bowl.
4. Drain all but 1 tablespoon of oil from pan. Stir in chickpeas and half the spice mixture; cook, stirring, for 30 seconds or until mixture is grainy. Transfer to large bowl. Mix pappadums, rice flakes, peas, noodles, sultanas, currants and remaining spice mixture into chickpea mixture.

makes about 6 cups

vegetable oil, for shallow-frying
4 plain pappadums
1 cup (100g) rice flakes (raw rolled rice)
1 cup (200g) roasted chickpeas
100g packet quick-dried prepared peas
100g packet ready-to-serve fried noodles
¼ cup (40g) sultanas
¼ cup (35g) currants

SPICE MIXTURE
2 tablespoons sugar
1 teaspoon salt
1 teaspoon ground cumin
½ teaspoon ground turmeric
¾ teaspoon chilli powder

Cook pappadums, one at a time, until puffed and crisp.

Cook rice flakes in same pan, stirring, until browned lightly.

Cook peanuts, stirring, in heated frying pan until browned lightly.

Cook spices in same pan, stirring, until fragrant.

spicy mixed nuts

2 tablespoons vegetable oil

1 cup (150g) raw peanuts

1 cup (150g) raw cashews

1 cup (150g) shelled pistachios

1 cup (160g) blanched almonds

2 teaspoons garam masala

½ teaspoon hot chilli powder

1 teaspoon salt

1 Heat oil in frying pan; cook the peanuts, stirring, until browned lightly; drain on absorbent paper. Repeat with remaining nuts.

2 Cook spices in same pan, stirring, until fragrant. Combine spices with nuts and salt in large bowl; cool.

makes about 4 cups

dhal and spinach soup

1. Cook cumin and coriander seeds, stirring, in dry frying pan until fragrant. Blend or process until crushed.
2. Heat ghee in large saucepan; cook onions, garlic, ginger, chillies, curry leaves, mustard and fenugreek seeds, stirring until onions are browned lightly. Add crushed spices, turmeric and asafoetida; cook, stirring, 1 minute.
3. Add dhal, potatoes and stock to pan; bring to boil then simmer, covered, 15 minutes or until potatoes are tender. Stir in spinach; cook 2 minutes.
4. Blend or process soup mixture, in batches, until smooth; return to pan.
5. Add tamarind and blended coconut milk powder and water; stir until soup is thoroughly heated through.

serves 6 to 8

2 teaspoons cumin seeds
2 teaspoons coriander seeds
1 tablespoon ghee
2 medium onions (300g), chopped
2 cloves garlic, crushed
1 tablespoon grated fresh ginger
2 dried red chillies, chopped
8 curry leaves, torn
2 teaspoons black mustard seeds
½ teaspoon fenugreek seeds
1 teaspoon ground turmeric
tiny pinch asafoetida powder
1 cup (200g) masoor dhal (red lentils), rinsed, drained
2 medium potatoes (400g), chopped
1.25 litres (5 cups) chicken stock
1kg spinach, roughly chopped
2 tablespoons tamarind concentrate
¾ cup (100g) coconut milk powder
1 cup (250ml) boiling water

Blend or process dry-roasted cumin and coriander seeds until crushed.

Cook spices and onion mixture, stirring, 1 minute.

Stir chopped spinach into soup; cook 2 minutes.

SOUPS & SNACKS

meat and vegetable samosas

1½ cups (225g) plain flour
2 teaspoons salt
2 tablespoons vegetable oil
⅓ cup (80ml) warm water, approximately
vegetable oil, for deep-frying

CHILLI, MINT AND BEEF FILLING
2 tablespoons vegetable oil
1 medium onion (150g), chopped
2 cloves garlic, crushed
2 teaspoons grated fresh ginger
½ teaspoon dried chilli flakes
2 teaspoons ground coriander
2 teaspoons garam masala
1 teaspoon ground turmeric
1 teaspoon sweet paprika
500g minced beef
2 tablespoons lemon juice
¼ cup chopped fresh mint

KUMARA AND CORIANDER FILLING
3 small kumaras (750g)
1 tablespoon vegetable oil
1 medium onion (150g), chopped
2 teaspoons cumin seeds
½ teaspoon black mustard seeds
1 long green chilli, chopped
2 cloves garlic, crushed
2 teaspoons grated fresh ginger
¼ teaspoon ground nutmeg
1 tablespoon lime juice
¼ cup chopped fresh coriander

The pastry and each filling is enough for 28 samosas.

1 Sift flour and salt into medium bowl; make well in the centre of flour, then add the 2 tablespoons of oil with just enough water to make a firm dough.
2 Knead dough on floured surface until smooth and elastic; form into a ball. Cover with plastic wrap; stand at room temperature for 30 minutes.
3 Meanwhile, make chilli, mint and beef filling or make kumara and coriander filling.
4 Divide dough into 14 equal pieces; roll each piece into a 14cm x 20cm oval, then cut oval in half widthways. Repeat process, keeping the remaining pieces covered to prevent drying out.
5 Brush edges of each half-oval with a little water; fold into cone shape. Fill with heaped tablespoon of filling; press edges together to seal. Repeat with remaining dough and filling.
6 Deep-fry samosas in hot oil, in batches, until browned and crisp; drain on absorbent paper.

CHILLI, MINT AND BEEF FILLING Heat oil in large frying pan; cook onion, stirring, until browned lightly. Add garlic, ginger, chilli and spices; cook, stirring, until fragrant. Add mince; cook, stirring, until well browned. Remove from heat, stir in juice and mint; cool.

KUMARA AND CORIANDER FILLING Cook kumaras until just tender, drain; cool. Cut each kumara into 1cm pieces. Heat oil in frying pan; cook onion, stirring, until soft. Add seeds, chilli, garlic, ginger and nutmeg; cook, stirring, until fragrant. Remove from heat, stir in kumara, juice and coriander; cool.

makes 28

Brush each oval half with a little water; fold into cone shape.

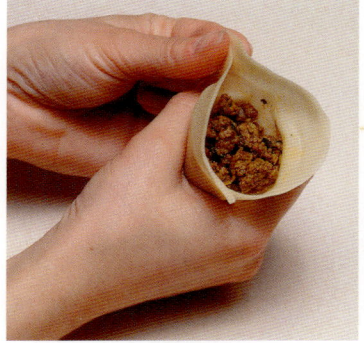
Fill pastry cone with filling; press edges together to seal.

Deep-fry samosas, in batches, until browned and crisp.

crunchy potatoes bengali-style

1. Boil, steam or microwave potatoes until almost tender; drain.
2. Heat ghee in small frying pan; cook panch phora, stirring, until fragrant. Add garlic, ginger, chilli and cumin; cook, stirring, 1 minute. Remove from heat.
3. Heat half the extra ghee in large frying pan; add half the potatoes, stir gently 5 minutes or until browned and crisp. Remove from pan; repeat with remaining ghee and potatoes.
4. Return potatoes, with spice mixture, salt, pepper and juice, to pan; stir until just heated through. Just before serving, sprinkle with fresh coriander.

serves 6

1.5kg potatoes, chopped
1 tablespoon ghee
1 tablespoon panch phora
3 cloves garlic, crushed
1 tablespoon grated fresh ginger
1 small red chilli, chopped
1 tablespoon ground cumin
3 tablespoons ghee, extra
1 teaspoon salt
1 teaspoon cracked black pepper
¼ cup (60ml) lemon juice
¼ cup chopped fresh coriander

Cook spices, garlic, ginger and chilli, stirring, 1 minute.

Cook potatoes with extra ghee, in batches, until browned and crisp.

Stir potatoes, spice mixture, salt, pepper and juice until heated.

mulligatawny soup

- 1 tablespoon ghee
- 1 large onion (200g), chopped
- 4 cloves garlic, crushed
- 2 teaspoons finely grated fresh ginger
- 2 small green chillies, chopped finely
- ¼ teaspoon ground cinnamon
- ¼ teaspoon ground cloves
- 2 teaspoons ground coriander
- 1½ teaspoons ground cumin
- 1 teaspoon ground turmeric
- 4 cardamom pods, bruised
- 5 curry leaves
- 1 medium carrot (120g), chopped
- 1 medium apple (150g), chopped
- 1 large potato (300g), chopped
- 1 cup (200g) masoor dhal (red lentils), rinsed, drained
- 1 litre (4 cups) chicken stock
- 1 tablespoon tamarind concentrate
- 1 tablespoon lemon juice
- 2 cups (500ml) coconut milk
- 2 tablespoons chopped fresh coriander

1 Heat ghee in large saucepan, add onion, garlic, ginger, chillies, all spices and curry leaves; cook, stirring, until onion is browned lightly and mixture is fragrant.
2 Add carrot, apple, potato, dhal and stock to pan; simmer, covered, 15 minutes or until vegetables are just tender. Discard pods and leaves.
3 Blend or process soup mixture, in batches, until smooth; return to pan. Add tamarind, juice, coconut milk and coriander; stir until heated through.

serves 6

Cook onion mixture, spices and curry leaves until onion browns.

Simmer soup until vegetables are just tender.

Blend or process soup, in batches, until smooth.

aloo tikka

1. Put dhal in bowl, cover with water, soak 45 minutes; drain.
2. Meanwhile, make tamarind sauce.
3. Place dhal in medium saucepan, cover with cold water; bring to boil, then immediately simmer, uncovered, 10 minutes or until just tender. Drain.
4. Boil, steam or microwave potatoes until tender; drain, then mash. Cool.
5. Combine mashed potatoes, besan, herbs, spices, chillies, egg yolk, juice and salt in large bowl; stir in dhal. Mould mixture into balls then flatten to form patties. Dust patties with extra besan, shake away excess.
6. Heat ghee in large non-stick frying pan; dip patties, one at a time, in egg. Cook until browned; drain on absorbent paper. Serve patties with tamarind sauce.

TAMARIND SAUCE Combine water and tamarind in small bowl; stand 30 minutes. Strain tamarind into small saucepan, pressing pulp to extract all liquid; discard tamarind pulp. Add ginger, cumin and jaggery to pan; bring to boil, then immediately simmer, uncovered, 5 minutes or until sauce thickens slightly. Strain sauce, serve warm.

serves 6 to 8

1/3 cup (65g) toor dhal (yellow split peas)
3 large (900g) potatoes, chopped
1/2 cup (75g) besan (chickpea flour)
1 tablespoon chopped fresh mint
1 tablespoon chopped fresh coriander
2 teaspoons garam masala
1 teaspoon ground cumin
1 teaspoon ground coriander
2 small red chillies, chopped finely
1 egg yolk
1 tablespoon lemon juice
2 teaspoons salt
besan, extra
3 tablespoons ghee
1 egg, beaten lightly

TAMARIND SAUCE

1 cup (250ml) boiling water
50g dried tamarind, chopped
2 teaspoons grated fresh ginger
1 teaspoon ground cumin
50g jaggery, chopped

Strain tamarind mixture into a small saucepan.

Bring dhal and water to the boil; simmer 10 minutes.

Mould mashed potato mixture into patties; dust with extra besan.

VEGETARIAN

vegetable and lentil sambar

1. Put dhal in bowl, cover with water, soak 1 hour; drain.
2. Heat oil in large saucepan; cook onion, stirring, until browned lightly. Add all spices, curry leaves and salt; cook, stirring, until fragrant.
3. Blend or process undrained crushed tomatoes, coconut, jaggery, tamarind and mustard seeds until smooth.
4. Add tomato mixture and dhal to onion mixture; boil, then immediately simmer, covered, 10 minutes.
5. Add potatoes, kumara and carrots; simmer, covered, 15 minutes. Add remaining ingredients; simmer, covered, 10 minutes or until vegetables are just tender.

serves 6 to 8

1 cup (200g) toor dhal (yellow split peas)

2 tablespoons vegetable oil

1 large onion (200g), sliced

1 tablespoon ground ginger

2 teaspoons ground cumin

2 teaspoons ground coriander

1 teaspoon ground turmeric

6 cardamom pods, bruised

8 curry leaves

1 teaspoon salt

2 x 400g cans tomatoes

½ cup (35g) shredded coconut

40g jaggery

1 tablespoon tamarind concentrate

1 tablespoon yellow mustard seeds

1kg small new potatoes, halved

500g kumara, chopped

2 medium carrots (240g), chopped

4 medium zucchini (480g), chopped

½ cup (125ml) water

1 tablespoon lime juice

Drain soaked dhal in seive over medium bowl.

Stir spices and curry leaves with onion until fragrant.

Add zucchini and remaining ingredients to pan.

VEGETARIAN

spiced snake beans

1. Heat ghee in wok or large frying pan; cook garlic, ginger, chillies and seeds, stirring, 2 minutes.
2. Add beans; cook, stirring, 5 minutes or until beans are just tender. Add coconut milk; cook, stirring, 5 minutes or until most of the liquid has evaporated. Just before serving, stir in coriander.

serves 4 to 6

2 tablespoons ghee
2 cloves garlic, crushed
1 tablespoon finely grated fresh ginger
2 small red chillies, chopped finely
2 teaspoons coriander seeds
1 teaspoon black mustard seeds
½ teaspoon fenugreek seeds
560g snake beans
½ cup (125ml) coconut milk
2 tablespoons chopped fresh coriander

Cook garlic, ginger, chillies and seeds in wok, stirring, 2 minutes.

Stir coconut milk and bean mixture, until almost all liquid evaporates.

Simmer potatoes in spicy coconut milk mixture until just tender.

cauliflower, pea and potato bhaji

2 tablespoons ghee

1 large onion (200g), sliced

2 cloves garlic, crushed

1 tablespoon sweet paprika

2 teaspoons garam masala

2 teaspoons ground cumin

6 cardamom pods, bruised

4 cloves

4 medium potatoes (800g), unpeeled, quartered

8 curry leaves

⅓ cup (30g) shredded coconut

½ cup (125ml) water

400ml can coconut milk

2 teaspoons salt

1 small cauliflower (1kg), chopped

1 cup (125g) frozen peas

1 Heat ghee in medium saucepan; cook onion and garlic, stirring, until onion is browned lightly. Add all spices; cook, stirring, until fragrant.
2 Add potatoes to pan with curry leaves, coconut, water, coconut milk and salt; simmer, covered, 15 minutes or until potatoes are just tender.
3 Add cauliflower to pan; simmer, covered, 10 minutes or until cauliflower is just tender. Stir in peas; simmer until peas are heated through.

serves 4 to 6

cheese kofta in creamy tomato sauce

1. Boil, steam or microwave potatoes until tender. Drain, then mash; cool.
2. Combine potatoes, cheese, eggs, flour, coriander, cumin and salt in medium bowl; refrigerate 30 minutes or until firm.
3. Meanwhile, make creamy tomato sauce.
4. Mould rounded tablespoons of mashed potato mixture into kofta shapes.
5. Just before cooking, toss kofta in cornflour; shake away any excess cornflour. Shallow-fry kofta in hot oil, in batches, until browned lightly; drain on absorbent paper. Serve immediately with creamy tomato sauce.

CREAMY TOMATO SAUCE Heat ghee in large saucepan; cook onions, stirring, until browned lightly. Add garlic, ginger and all spices; cook, stirring, until fragrant. Add tomatoes, nuts and water; boil, then immediately simmer, uncovered, 20 minutes or until mixture is slightly thickened. Blend or process tomato mixture until smooth. Just before serving, return to pan; add cream and salt, stir until heated through.

serves 4 to 6

500g potatoes, chopped
2½ cups (500g) ricotta cheese
2 eggs, beaten lightly
⅓ cup (50g) plain flour
¼ cup chopped fresh coriander
1 teaspoon ground cumin
1 teaspoon salt
cornflour, for dusting
vegetable oil, for shallow-frying

CREAMY TOMATO SAUCE
2 tablespoons ghee
2 medium onions (300g), chopped
4 cloves garlic, chopped
2 tablespoons grated fresh ginger
2 teaspoons garam masala
1 teaspoon coriander seeds
2 teaspoons ground sweet paprika
1 teaspoon ground cumin
4 large tomatoes (1kg), peeled, seeded, chopped
1 cup (150g) cashews, toasted, chopped
1 cup (250ml) water
300ml cream
1 teaspoon salt

Simmer tomato and onion mixture until thickened.

Mould rounded tablespoons of potato mixture into kofta shapes.

Shallow-fry kofta, in batches, until browned lightly.

Simmer pumpkin, cream and onion mixture until pumpkin is tender.

Simmer spinach and pumpkin curry until spinach wilts.

spinach and pumpkin curry

1 Peel pumpkin; cut into 3cm pieces.
2 Heat ghee in large saucepan; cook onions, stirring, until browned lightly. Add garlic, ginger, chillies and spices; cook, stirring, until fragrant.
3 Add pumpkin pieces and cream; simmer, covered, 20 minutes or until pumpkin is just tender.
4 Add spinach, curry leaves and coriander; simmer until spinach is just wilted. Just before serving, sprinkle with flaked almonds.

serves 4

1kg pumpkin

2 tablespoons ghee

2 medium onions (300g), sliced

2 cloves garlic, crushed

1 teaspoon grated fresh ginger

2 small green chillies, sliced thinly

1 teaspoon ground coriander

1 teaspoon ground cumin

1 teaspoon black mustard seeds

½ teaspoon ground turmeric

300ml cream

250g spinach, chopped roughly

3 curry leaves, torn

2 tablespoons chopped fresh coriander

1 tablespoon flaked almonds, toasted

spicy okra

- 2 tablespoons vegetable oil
- 2 medium onions (300g), sliced
- 1 tablespoon cumin seeds
- 4 cloves garlic, crushed
- 2 long green chillies, chopped
- 4 curry leaves
- 2 teaspoons ground coriander
- 1 teaspoon ground turmeric
- ½ teaspoon ground sweet paprika
- ½ teaspoon ground ginger
- 1kg okra
- 1 cup (250ml) water
- ¼ cup (60ml) tomato paste
- 2 tablespoons white vinegar
- 2 teaspoons sugar
- ¼ cup firmly packed fresh coriander leaves
- ½ teaspoon garam masala

1 Heat oil in large frying pan; cook onions, stirring, until browned lightly. Add the seeds; cook, stirring, until seeds start to pop. Add garlic, chillies, curry leaves, ground coriander, turmeric, paprika and ginger; cook, stirring, until fragrant.

2 Add okra, stir to coat in the spice mixture. Add water, paste, vinegar and sugar; boil, then immediately simmer, covered, 30 minutes, stirring occasionally, or until okra is tender. Just before serving, stir in fresh coriander and sprinkle with garam masala.

serves 4 to 6

Cook onion mixture, garlic, chillies, leaves and all spices until fragrant.

Simmer okra in onion and tomato mixture until okra is tender.

VEGETARIAN

mixed vegetable curry

1 Combine yogurt, garlic, ginger, salt, pepper and spices in small bowl; stand 15 minutes. Roughly chop potatoes.
2 Heat ghee and oil together in large saucepan; cook onions, stirring, until onions are browned lightly. Add potatoes, carrot, cauliflower, eggplants and bay leaves; cook, stirring, 5 minutes.
3 Add yogurt mixture, water and coconut cream; simmer, covered, 15 minutes or until potatoes are just tender.
4 Add beans; simmer, uncovered, further 5 minutes or until beans are just tender. Just before serving, sprinkle with chopped mint.

serves 4

¼ cup (60ml) yogurt
2 cloves garlic, crushed
2 teaspoons grated fresh ginger
1 teaspoon salt
¼ teaspoon cracked black pepper
1 teaspoon ground coriander
1 teaspoon chilli powder
½ teaspoon garam masala
4 cardamom pods, bruised
2 medium potatoes (400g)
3 tablespoons ghee
1 tablespoon vegetable oil
2 medium onions (300g), sliced
1 large carrot (180g), sliced
300g cauliflower florets
2 baby eggplants (120g), sliced
2 bay leaves
½ cup (125ml) water
1 cup (250ml) coconut cream
150g green beans, halved
2 tablespoons chopped fresh mint

Combine yogurt, garlic, ginger, salt, pepper and spices in small bowl.

Add vegetables and bay leaves to onion mixture; cook 5 minutes.

Rinse each dhal, separately, under cold water; drain.

mixed dhal

½ cup (100g) toor dhal (yellow split peas)

½ cup (100g) masoor dhal (red lentils)

½ cup (100g) moong dhal (split mung beans)

2 tablespoons ghee

3 teaspoons black mustard seeds

½ teaspoon kalonji (black onion seeds)

2 medium onions (300g), chopped

4 cloves garlic, crushed

1 tablespoon grated fresh ginger

1 tablespoon ground cumin

3 teaspoons ground coriander

1 teaspoon ground turmeric

1 teaspoon chilli powder

2 x 400g cans tomatoes

2½ cups (625ml) vegetable stock

½ teaspoon cracked black pepper

⅓ cup (80ml) cream

2 tablespoons chopped fresh coriander

1 Rinse each dhal, separately, under cold water; drain. Put only the toor dhal in small bowl, cover with water; soak 30 minutes, drain.
2 Heat ghee in large heavy-based saucepan; cook seeds, stirring, until they start to pop. Add onions, garlic and ginger; cook, stirring, until onions are browned lightly.
3 Add ground spices; cook, stirring, 1 minute. Add all dhal, undrained crushed tomatoes and stock; simmer, covered, 30 minutes or until masoor dhal are tender. Just before serving, add remaining ingredients; stir over low heat until just heated through.

serves 4 to 6

Cook soaked chickpeas in boiling water until tender.

channa dhal

1. Place chickpeas in medium bowl, cover with water; soak overnight, drain. Boil or microwave chickpeas in water, until tender; drain.
2. Heat oil in large saucepan; cook onion, stirring, until onion is browned lightly. Add ginger, garlic, spices and seeds; cook, stirring, until fragrant.
3. Add undrained crushed tomatoes, coconut cream, salt and chickpeas; cook, stirring, 5 minutes or until thickened.

serves 4 to 6

1½ cups (300g) dried chickpeas
2 tablespoons vegetable oil
1 medium onion (150g), chopped finely
1 teaspoon grated fresh ginger
3 cloves garlic, crushed
2 teaspoons garam masala
2 teaspoons ground cumin
2 teaspoons ground coriander
2 teaspoons sweet paprika
½ teaspoon chilli powder
¼ teaspoon ground turmeric
1 teaspoon yellow mustard seeds
400g can tomatoes
2 tablespoons coconut cream
2 teaspoons salt

VEGETARIAN

brinjal mollee

40g dried tamarind

½ cup (125ml) boiling water

3 small eggplants (690g), sliced

2 teaspoons salt

2 tablespoons vegetable oil

2 large onions (400g), sliced

2 cloves garlic, crushed

2 teaspoons finely grated fresh ginger

6 curry leaves

3 small red chillies, chopped finely

2 teaspoons yellow mustard seeds

2 teaspoons cumin seeds

2 teaspoons ground coriander

2 tablespoons tomato paste

1½ cups (375ml) water

½ cup (125ml) coconut cream

1 tablespoon chopped fresh coriander

1 Combine tamarind and boiling water in small bowl; stand 30 minutes. Strain tamarind over small bowl, pressing to extract as much liquid as possible. Discard tamarind.
2 Sprinkle eggplant slices, both sides, with salt; drain in colander 30 minutes. Rinse eggplant under cold water; drain.
3 Heat oil in medium saucepan; cook onions, garlic and ginger, stirring, until onions are browned lightly. Add curry leaves, chillies, seeds and ground coriander; cook, stirring, until mixture is fragrant.
4 Add tamarind liquid, paste, water and coconut cream; bring to the boil. Add eggplant; simmer, covered, 15 minutes or until eggplant is very soft. Remove cover; simmer 5 minutes or until sauce is thickened. Just before serving, sprinkle with fresh coriander.

serves 4

Strain tamarind over small bowl, pressing to extract liquid.

Drain salted eggplant slices in colander 30 minutes.

SEAFOOD

prawns dhania masala

1. Shell and devein prawns, leaving tails intact.
2. Blend or process all masala paste ingredients until smooth.
3. Heat oil in large saucepan; cook onion, stirring, until browned lightly.
4. Add masala paste to pan; cook, stirring, until fragrant. Stir in prawns; cook 5 minutes or until tender.

serves 4 to 6

1.5kg uncooked king prawns
2 tablespoons vegetable oil
1 large onion (200g), sliced

MASALA PASTE

⅔ cup firmly packed fresh coriander leaves
⅓ cup firmly packed fresh mint leaves
2 tablespoons water
2 teaspoons sesame oil
2 cloves garlic, chopped
1 tablespoon chopped fresh ginger
2 tablespoons white vinegar
1 teaspoon ground turmeric
1 teaspoon ground cumin
1 teaspoon chilli powder
1 teaspoon ground fennel
½ teaspoon ground cardamom
1 teaspoon salt

Shell and devein prawns, leaving tails intact.

Process all masala paste ingredients until smooth.

Stir prawns into masala paste; cook until prawns are tender.

fish kofta

- 700g boneless white fish fillets, chopped
- 2 medium onions (300g), chopped
- ½ cup firmly packed fresh coriander leaves
- 2 large fresh chillies, chopped
- 1 tablespoon ghee
- 2 cloves garlic, crushed
- 2 teaspoons ground coriander
- 1 teaspoon ground cumin
- ½ teaspoon ground turmeric
- 2 cinnamon sticks
- 1 teaspoon ground fenugreek
- 3 medium tomatoes (570g), peeled, chopped

1. Bring large saucepan of water to the boil; add fish, immediately reduce heat to simmer, uncovered, until fish is just tender. Strain fish over large bowl; reserve 2 cups (500ml) cooking liquid.
2. Blend or process fish with half the onion, half the fresh coriander and all the chillies until just combined.
3. Mould rounded tablespoons of mixture into kofta shapes, place on tray; refrigerate 30 minutes.
4. Heat half the ghee in non-stick frying pan; cook kofta, in batches, until browned both sides; drain on absorbent paper.
5. Heat remaining ghee in large saucepan; cook remaining onion, the garlic and all spices, stirring, until onion is browned lightly. Add tomatoes; cook, stirring, 5 minutes or until tomatoes are very soft. Add reserved cooking liquid; simmer, uncovered, 10 minutes or until sauce is thickened.
6. Add kofta; simmer 5 minutes or until heated through. Just before serving, sprinkle with the remaining fresh coriander.

serves 4

Cook fish pieces in simmering water until just tender.

Process fish with half the onion, half the coriander and the chillies.

Place kofta-shaped fish mixture on a baking tray.

prawn patia

1 Shell and devein prawns, leaving tails intact.
2 Blend or process undrained crushed tomatoes, chillies, jaggery, tamarind, paste and fresh coriander until smooth.
3 Heat ghee in medium frying pan; cook onions and garlic, stirring, until onions are browned lightly. Add ground spices and chilli powder; cook, stirring, until fragrant.
4 Add tomato mixture to pan; bring to boil, then immediately simmer, uncovered, 10 minutes or until mixture thickens slightly. Add prawns; cook, stirring, 5 minutes or until prawns are tender. Just before serving, scatter with curry leaves.

serves 4

1.5kg uncooked medium prawns
400g can tomatoes
2 large green chillies, chopped
60g jaggery
1 tablespoon tamarind concentrate
¼ cup (60ml) tomato paste
⅓ cup firmly packed fresh coriander leaves
2 tablespoons ghee
2 large onions (400g), chopped
4 cloves garlic, crushed
2 teaspoons ground coriander
2 teaspoons garam masala
2 teaspoons ground cumin
1 teaspoon ground turmeric
1 teaspoon hot chilli powder
8 curry leaves

Shell and devein prawns, leaving tails intact.

Process tomatoes, chillies, jaggery, tamarind, paste and coriander.

Simmer tomato and onion mixture until slightly thickened.

goan fish curry

½ cup (35g) shredded coconut, toasted
2 cloves garlic, chopped
3 small red chillies, chopped
2 teaspoons coriander seeds
2 teaspoons cumin seeds
½ teaspoon ground turmeric
1 tablespoon tamarind concentrate
1 tablespoon finely grated fresh ginger
2 medium onions (300g), chopped
½ cup (125ml) cold water
2 tablespoons vegetable oil
2 medium tomatoes (380g), chopped
8 curry leaves
½ cup (125ml) chicken stock
⅔ cup (85g) coconut milk powder
⅔ cup (160ml) boiling water
1kg boneless white fish fillets, chopped

1. Blend or process coconut, garlic, chillies, seeds, turmeric, tamarind, ginger and half the onions with the cold water until pureed.
2. Heat oil in large saucepan; cook the remaining onion, stirring, until browned lightly. Add the coconut mixture; cook, stirring, until fragrant.
3. Add tomatoes, curry leaves and stock to pan with blended coconut milk powder and boiling water; simmer, uncovered, 10 minutes or until sauce is thickened.
4. Add fish; simmer, covered, 10 minutes or until fish is tender.

serves 4 to 6

Stir coconut mixture and onion mixture together until fragrant.

Add fish pieces to pan; simmer until pieces are tender.

SEAFOOD

fish makhanwala

1 Cut fish fillets into 4cm pieces.
2 Heat ghee in large frying pan; cook onion, stirring, until browned lightly. Add garlic, ginger, spices and salt; cook, stirring, until fragrant.
3 Add undrained crushed tomatoes, cream and juice; simmer, uncovered, 5 minutes or until the sauce is slightly thickened.
4 Add fish; simmer, covered, 10 minutes or until fish is tender. Just before serving, sprinkle with fresh coriander.

serves 4

750g thick boneless white fish fillets
2 tablespoons ghee
1 large onion (200g), sliced
4 cloves garlic, crushed
1 tablespoon grated fresh ginger
4 cardamom pods, bruised
2 teaspoons ground coriander
3 teaspoons ground cumin
½ teaspoon ground cinnamon
½ teaspoon cayenne pepper
1 teaspoon garam masala
2 teaspoons salt
2 x 400g cans tomatoes
½ cup (125ml) cream
1 tablespoon lemon juice
2 tablespoons chopped fresh coriander

Stir garlic, ginger, spices and salt into onion mixture.

Simmer fish pieces in creamy tomato mixture until tender.

Shell and devein prawns, leaving tails intact.

Stir ground spice mixture into cooked onion until fragrant.

prawn and green mango curry

1.5kg uncooked king prawns

2 tablespoons vegetable oil

1 large onion (200g), chopped finely

2 medium green mangoes (860g), peeled, sliced

8 curry leaves, torn

¼ cup (35g) coconut milk powder

2 cups (500ml) boiling water

⅓ cup (80 ml) cream

green onion, chopped, for garnish

SPICE MIXTURE

½ cup (45g) desiccated coconut, toasted

2 cloves garlic, chopped

½ teaspoon ground turmeric

2 teaspoons ground coriander

3 long dried red chillies, chopped

1 teaspoon salt

1 Shell and devein prawns, leaving tails intact.
2 Grind or process all spice mixture ingredients until crushed.
3 Heat oil in large saucepan; cook onion, stirring, until browned lightly. Add ground spice mixture; cook, stirring, until fragrant.
4 Add prawns, mango slices and curry leaves with blended coconut milk powder and boiling water; simmer, uncovered, 5 minutes or until prawns are tender. Remove from heat, stir in cream. Just before serving, sprinkle with chopped green onions.

serves 4 to 6

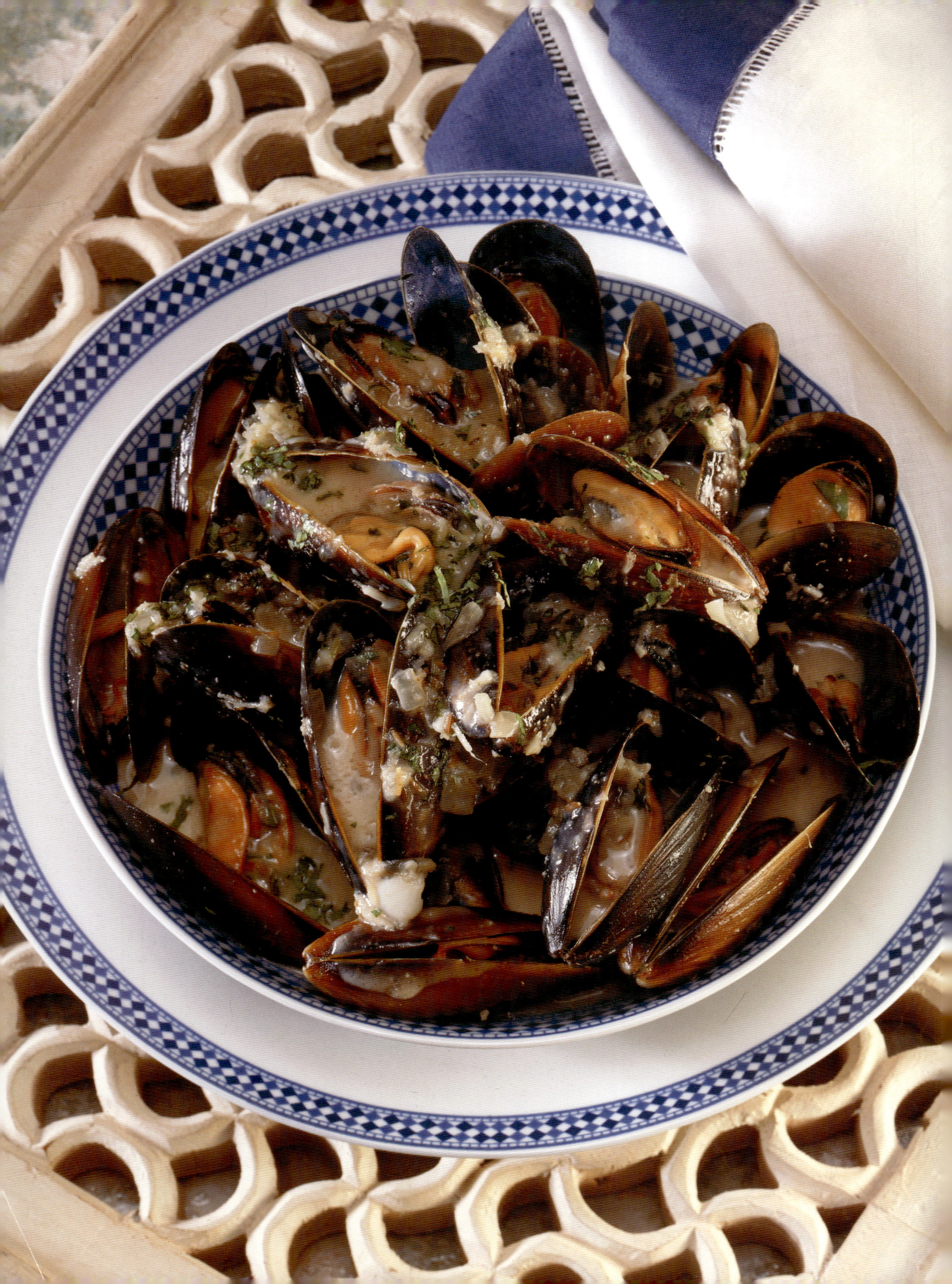

SEAFOOD

mussel masala

- 1.5kg small black mussels
- 2 tablespoons vegetable oil
- 1 medium onion (150g), chopped finely
- 1 tablespoon finely grated fresh ginger
- 4 cloves garlic, crushed
- 2 bay leaves
- 2 small green chillies, chopped finely
- 1 teaspoon cumin seeds
- ½ teaspoon cloves
- 6 cardamom pods, bruised
- 2 teaspoons ground coriander
- 1 teaspoon sugar
- 400ml can coconut cream
- ¼ cup (60ml) water
- 2 tablespoons chopped fresh coriander

1 Scrub mussels; remove beards from the shells.
2 Heat oil in saucepan; cook onion, ginger and garlic, stirring, until onion is soft.
3 Add bay leaves, chillies, seeds and all spices; cook, stirring, until fragrant.
4 Stir in sugar, coconut cream and water; simmer, uncovered, 10 minutes or until sauce is thickened. Add mussels; simmer, covered, 3 minutes or until mussels open. Discard any unopened mussels. Just before serving, sprinkle with fresh coriander.

serves 4

Scrub mussels well and remove the beards.

Stir in bay leaves, chillies, seeds and spices to onion mixture.

POULTRY

chicken tikka

1. Cut chicken fillets in half; make three shallow cuts across each piece.
2. Combine remaining ingredients in large bowl, add chicken pieces; toss chicken to coat with marinade. Cover; refrigerate overnight.
3. Barbecue or griddle-fry chicken, both sides, until tender.

serves 4 to 6

6 single chicken breast fillets (1kg)
1 tablespoon grated fresh ginger
3 cloves garlic, crushed
2 tablespoons lemon juice
2 teaspoons ground coriander
2 teaspoons ground cumin
½ teaspoon garam masala
½ teaspoon chilli powder
⅓ cup (80ml) yogurt
2 tablespoons tomato paste
pinch tandoori-coloured powder

Cut fillets in half; make three cuts across each piece.

Coat chicken in combined remaining ingredients; refrigerate.

Cook chicken pieces, both sides, until tender.

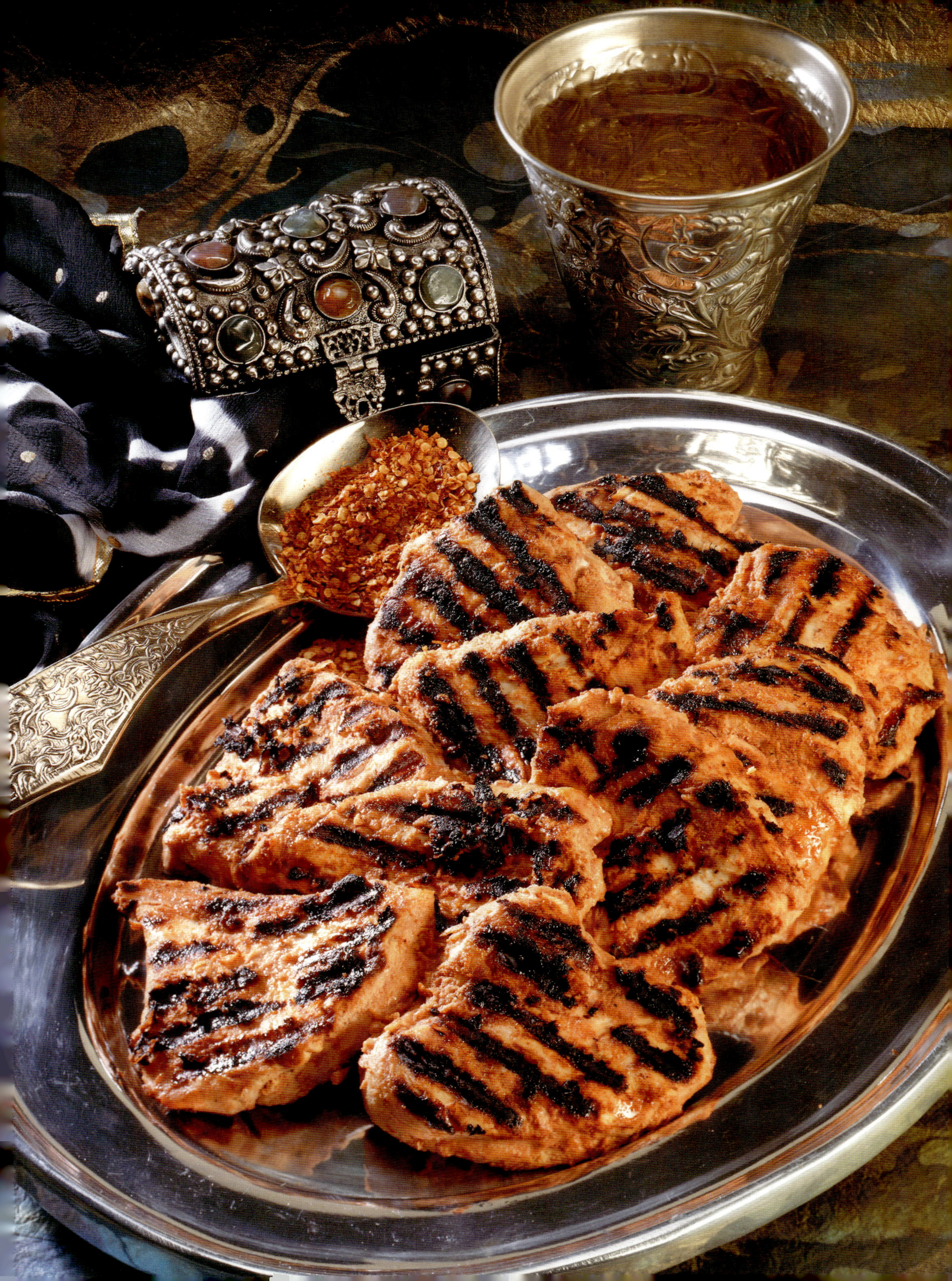

Toss chicken to coat in marinade ingredients; refrigerate overnight.

Add chicken and marinade to onion mixture; cook 5 minutes.

butter chicken

1. Cut chicken fillets into three pieces.
2. Combine ground spices, garlic, ginger, vinegar, paste and yogurt in large bowl, add chicken; toss chicken to coat in marinade. Cover; refrigerate overnight.
3. Finely chop onion. Heat butter in large saucepan, add onion, cinnamon and cardamom; cook, stirring, until onion is browned lightly. Add chicken marinade mixture; cook, stirring, 5 minutes.
4. Add salt, paprika, puree and stock; simmer, uncovered, 10 minutes, stirring occasionally. Add cream; simmer 10 minutes or until chicken is tender.

serves 4 to 6

6 single chicken breast fillets (1kg)
2 teaspoons garam masala
2 teaspoons ground coriander
¾ teaspoon chilli powder
3 cloves garlic, crushed
2 teaspoons grated fresh ginger
2 tablespoons white vinegar
¼ cup (60ml) tomato paste
½ cup (125ml) yogurt
1 large onion (200g)
80g butter
1 cinnamon stick
4 cardamom pods, bruised
1 teaspoon salt
3 teaspoons sweet paprika
425g can tomato puree
¾ cup (180ml) chicken stock
1 cup (250ml) cream

south indian chicken curry

2 tablespoons vegetable oil
2 teaspoons black mustard seeds
¼ teaspoon fenugreek seeds
16 curry leaves, torn
2 large onions (400g), chopped finely
3 cloves garlic, crushed
1 tablespoon grated fresh ginger
1 small red chilli, chopped
1 tablespoon ground coriander
2 teaspoons ground sweet paprika
1 teaspoon ground turmeric
¾ teaspoon ground fennel
1 teaspoon salt
10 chicken thigh cutlets (1.6kg), skin removed
400g can tomatoes
¼ cup (60ml) chicken stock
300g snake beans
1¼ cups (310ml) coconut cream
1 tablespoon tamarind concentrate

1. Heat oil in large saucepan; cook seeds and curry leaves, stirring, until fragrant. Add onions, garlic, ginger and chilli; cook, stirring, until onions are browned lightly.
2. Add ground spices and salt; cook, stirring, 1 minute.
3. Add chicken to pan along with undrained crushed tomatoes and stock; simmer, covered, 30 minutes. Remove lid; simmer 20 minutes or until sauce is thickened slightly.
4. Add beans to pan along with cream and tamarind; simmer, uncovered, 10 minutes or until beans are tender.

serves 4 to 6

Cook seeds and leaves, stir in onions, garlic, ginger and chilli.

Simmer chicken in tomato mixture until thickened.

masala chicken drumsticks

1 Grind or process coriander, cumin and cardamom seeds until crushed.
2 Place crushed seeds with spices in a dry frying pan; stir over heat until fragrant. Remove from heat. Add oil and water, stir until combined.
3 Make diagonal cuts, about 1cm apart, through to the bone, on both sides of drumsticks.
4 Rub spice mixture all over the drumsticks, place in shallow dish; cover, refrigerate 6 hours or overnight.
5 Cook drumsticks on a heated oiled griddle pan (or barbecue or grill) until browned and cooked through.

serves 4

2 teaspoons coriander seeds
2 teaspoons cumin seeds
½ teaspoon cardamom seeds
½ teaspoon hot chilli powder
½ teaspoon ground black pepper
¼ teaspoon ground cinnamon
¼ teaspoon ground cloves
1 tablespoon vegetable oil
1 tablespoon water
8 chicken drumsticks (1.2kg)

Combine oil and water with dry roasted spices.

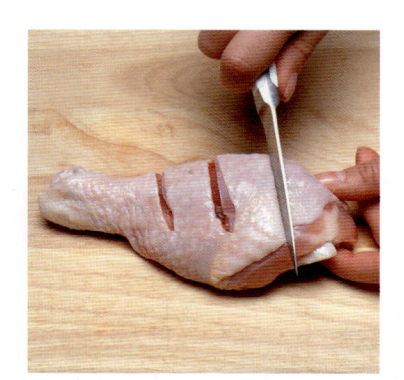

Make diagonal cuts through to the bone, on both sides of drumsticks.

Place spice-rubbed drumsticks in a shallow dish.

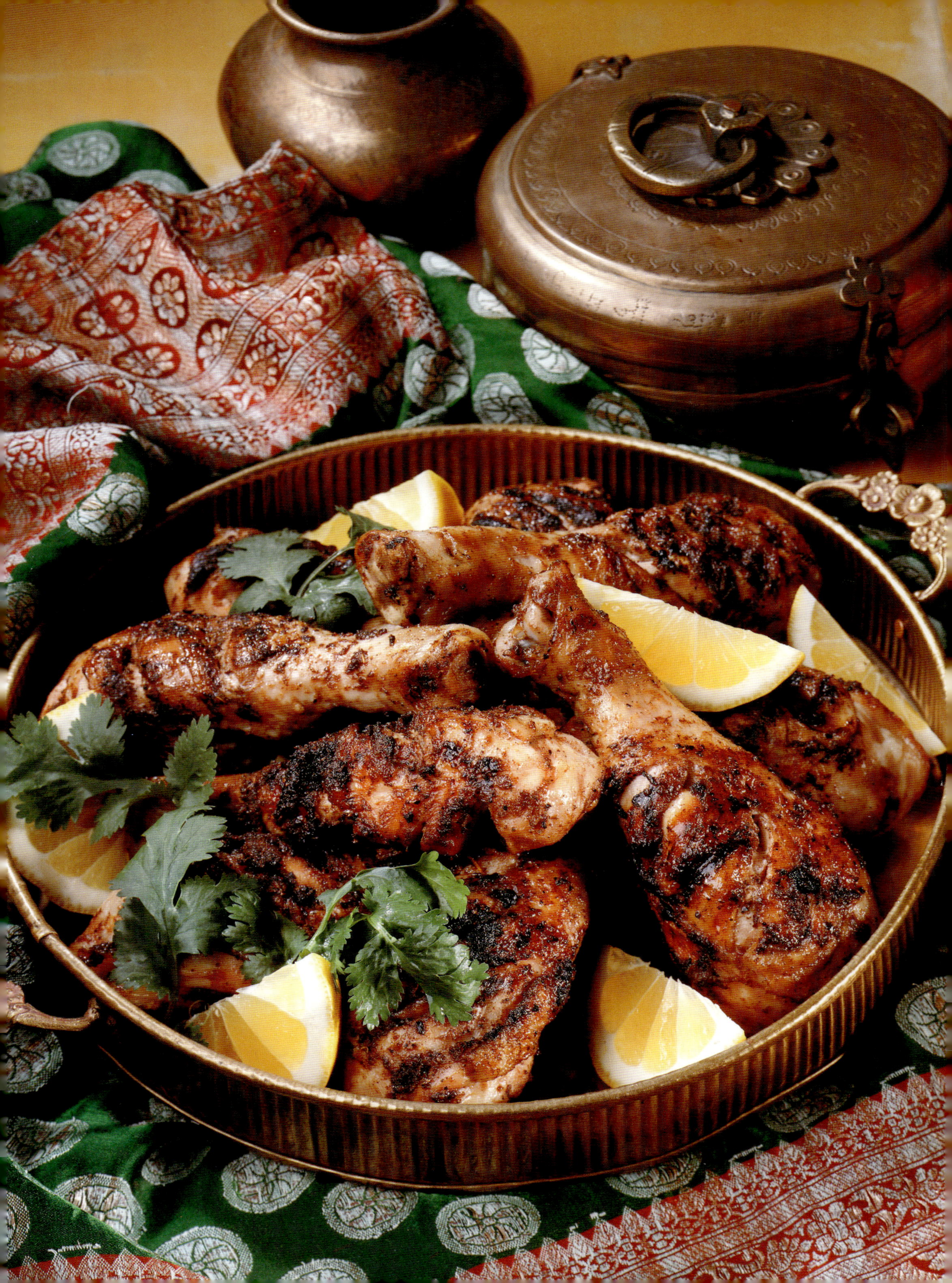

chicken with lentils and spinach

1. Place dhal in medium bowl, cover with cold water; stand 1 hour. Drain.
2. Remove and discard wing tip from each wing; cut wings in half at joint.
3. Cover tamarind with the boiling water in small bowl; stand 30 minutes. Strain over bowl, pressing tamarind to extract all liquid; discard tamarind.
4. Heat ghee in large saucepan; cook onions, stirring, until browned lightly. Add garlic, chillies, ginger and spices; stir until fragrant.
5. Add dhal to pan along with chicken, tamarind liquid, juice and jaggery; simmer, covered, 30 minutes or until chicken is tender. Add herbs and spinach; simmer, uncovered, 3 minutes or until spinach is wilted.

serves 6 to 8

1 cup (200g) toor dhal (yellow split peas)
18 chicken wings (1.5kg)
40g dried tamarind pulp
1½ cups (375ml) boiling water
2 tablespoons ghee
2 large onions (400g), sliced
2 cloves garlic, crushed
4 large green chillies, chopped
1 tablespoon grated fresh ginger
1 teaspoon ground turmeric
2 teaspoons garam masala
1 teaspoon ground fenugreek
2 tablespoons lime juice
30g jaggery
⅓ cup chopped fresh mint
⅓ cup chopped fresh coriander
500g spinach, chopped

Remove and discard wing tip; cut wings in half at joint.

Strain tamarind over bowl, pressing to extract all liquid.

POULTRY

red chicken curry

- 2 tablespoons ghee
- 2 medium onions (300g), sliced
- 4 cloves garlic, crushed
- 2 teaspoons finely grated fresh ginger
- 1 medium red capsicum (200g), chopped
- 2 teaspoons ground cumin
- 2 teaspoons ground coriander
- 2 teaspoons sweet paprika
- 1 teaspoon hot chilli powder
- 1 tablespoon tomato paste
- 425g can tomatoes
- 9 chicken thigh fillets (1kg)
- 2 cups (500ml) chicken stock
- ¼ cup (60ml) cream
- 1 tablespoon tamarind concentrate
- red food colouring, optional

1. Heat ghee in large saucepan, add onions, garlic, ginger, capsicum and spices; cook, stirring, until onions are browned lightly.
2. Add paste to pan along with undrained crushed tomatoes, chicken and stock; simmer, covered, 20 minutes or until chicken is cooked through.
3. Stir cream, tamarind and food colouring, if using, into curry. Simmer, uncovered, 15 minutes or until mixture has thickened slightly.

serves 4 to 6

Cook onions, garlic, ginger, capsicum and spices until onion browns lightly.

dry chicken curry

1. Heat ghee in large saucepan; cook onions, stirring, until browned lightly.
2. Add curry leaves to pan, along with seeds, garlic, ginger, ground spices, chilli powder and salt; cook, stirring, until fragrant. Add chicken; stir well to coat in spice mixture.
3. Pour in water; simmer, covered, 30 minutes or until chicken is tender. Boil, uncovered, 15 minutes or until almost all liquid has evaporated. Just before serving, stir in coriander.

serves 6

2 tablespoons ghee
2 medium onions (300g), chopped
6 curry leaves, torn
1 teaspoon cumin seeds
1 teaspoon black mustard seeds
2 cloves garlic, crushed
2 teaspoons grated fresh ginger
1 teaspoon garam masala
1 teaspoon ground turmeric
½ teaspoon chilli powder
1 teaspoon salt
9 chicken thigh fillets (1kg), halved
½ cup (125ml) water
1 tablespoon chopped fresh coriander

Add chicken to pan; stir well to coat in spice mixture.

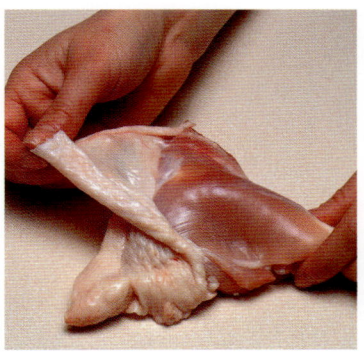

Remove skin from chicken drumsticks and thighs.

chicken chettinad

2 teaspoons black peppercorns
4 large dried red chillies
1 teaspoon fennel seeds
2 tablespoons white poppy seeds
¼ teaspoon cardmom seeds
4 chicken drumsticks (600g)
4 chicken thighs (880g)
2 tablespoons ghee
2 medium onions (300g), sliced
1 tablespoon grated fresh ginger
1 teaspoon hot chilli powder
¾ teaspoon grated nutmeg
¾ cup (180ml) water
400ml can coconut cream
¼ cup (60ml) tomato paste
6 curry leaves
2 star anise
1 tablespoon lime juice
2 medium tomatoes (380g), peeled, chopped

1 Grind or process black peppercorns, chillies and seeds until crushed.
2 Remove skin from chicken drumsticks and thighs.
3 Heat ghee in large saucepan; cook onions, stirring, occasionally, until browned lightly. Add ginger, chilli powder, nutmeg and crushed spices; cook, stirring, until fragrant.
4 Add chicken and remaining ingredients; simmer, covered, for 20 minutes. Remove cover; simmer 20 minutes or until chicken is tender and sauce thickened.

serves 4 to 6

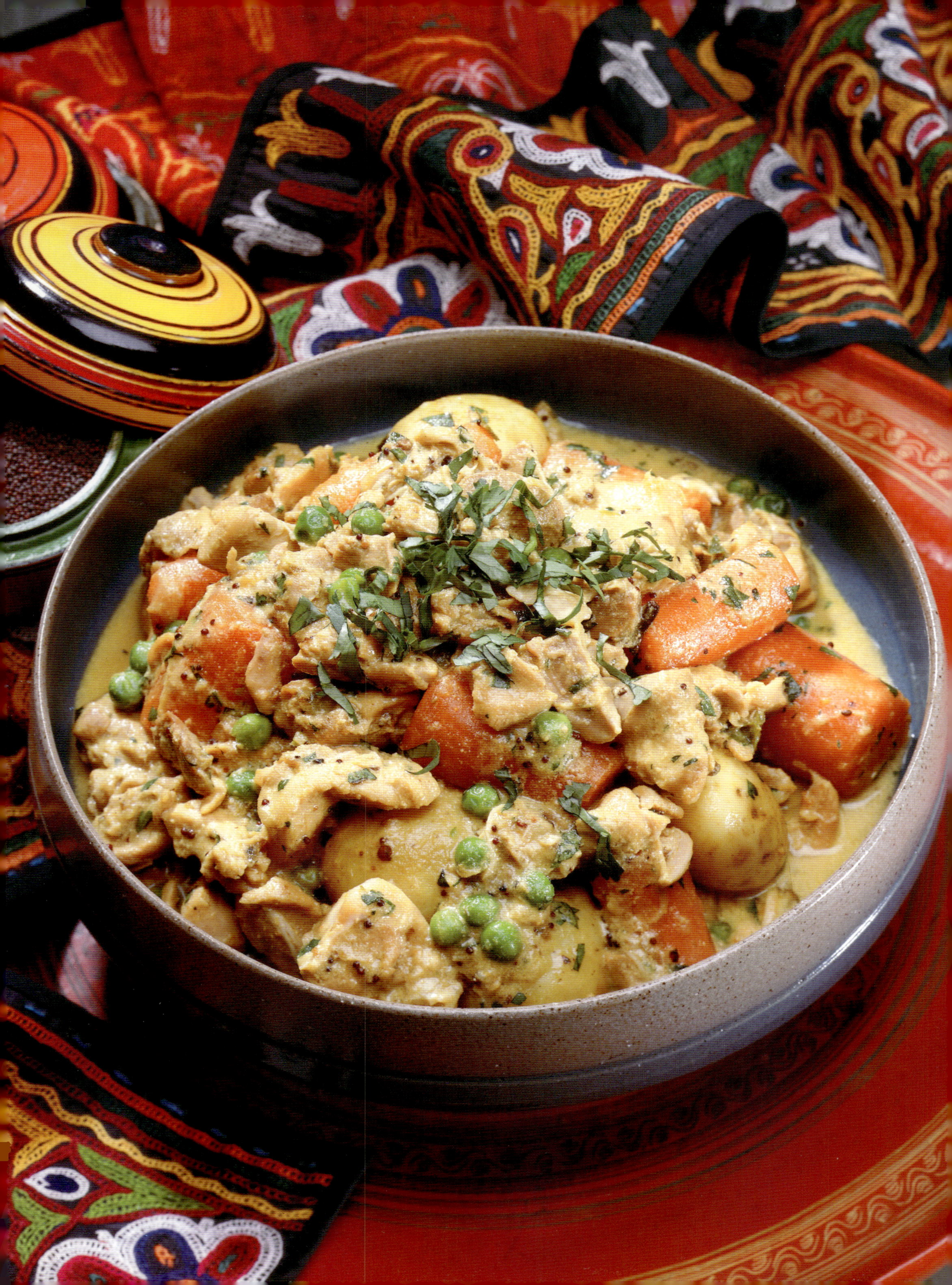

chicken ishtew

1 tablespoon vegetable oil
1 tablespoon ghee
1½ teaspoons black mustard seeds
1 cinnamon stick
2 teaspoons coriander seeds, crushed
3 cloves
4 cardamom pods, bruised
16 curry leaves, torn
2 bay leaves
1½ tablespoons finely chopped fresh ginger
1½ teaspoons cracked black pepper
1 large green chilli, chopped
3 cloves garlic, crushed
1 teaspoon salt
½ teaspoon ground turmeric
2 medium onions (300g), sliced thickly
1 teaspoon garam masala
11 chicken thigh fillets (1.2kg), halved
1⅓ cups (330ml) chicken stock
12 baby new potatoes (500g)
2 large carrots (360g), chopped roughly
¾ cup (100g) coconut milk powder
¾ cup (180ml) boiling water
½ cup (60g) frozen peas
2 tablespoons lemon juice
2 tablespoons chopped fresh coriander

1. Heat oil and ghee in large saucepan; cook mustard seeds, stirring, 30 seconds. Add whole spices, and curry and bay leaves; stir until fragrant.
2. Add ginger to pan along with black pepper, chilli, garlic, salt and turmeric; stir over heat 1 minute.
3. Add onions to pan; cook, stirring, until browned lightly. Add garam masala, chicken, stock, potatoes and carrots with blended coconut milk powder and water; simmer, covered, 45 minutes, stirring occasionally. Simmer, uncovered, 15 minutes.
4. Add remaining ingredients; simmer 5 minutes or until peas are just cooked through.

serves 6

Stir whole spices, curry leaves and bay leaves in ghee until fragrant.

Add peas, juice and fresh coriander to stew; simmer 5 minutes.

MEAT

tandoori lamb cutlets

1 Blend or process yogurt, onion, juice, oil, ginger, garlic, spices and tandoori-coloured powder until smooth.
2 Transfer yogurt mixture to large bowl, add lamb cutlets; toss cutlets to coat in marinade. Cover; refrigerate overnight.
3 Cook cutlets, in batches, on a heated oiled griddle pan (or grill or barbecue), until browned and tender.

serves 4

1 cup (250ml) yogurt

1 medium onion (150g), chopped

2 tablespoons lemon juice

1 tablespoon vegetable oil

1 tablespoon chopped fresh ginger

3 cloves garlic, chopped

2 teaspoons chilli powder

1 teaspoon garam masala

1 teaspoon ground cumin

tiny pinch tandoori-coloured powder

12 lamb cutlets

Process yogurt and remaining marinade ingredients until smooth.

Coat cutlets with yogurt marinade; cover, refrigerate overnight.

Cook cutlets, in batches, until browned and tender.

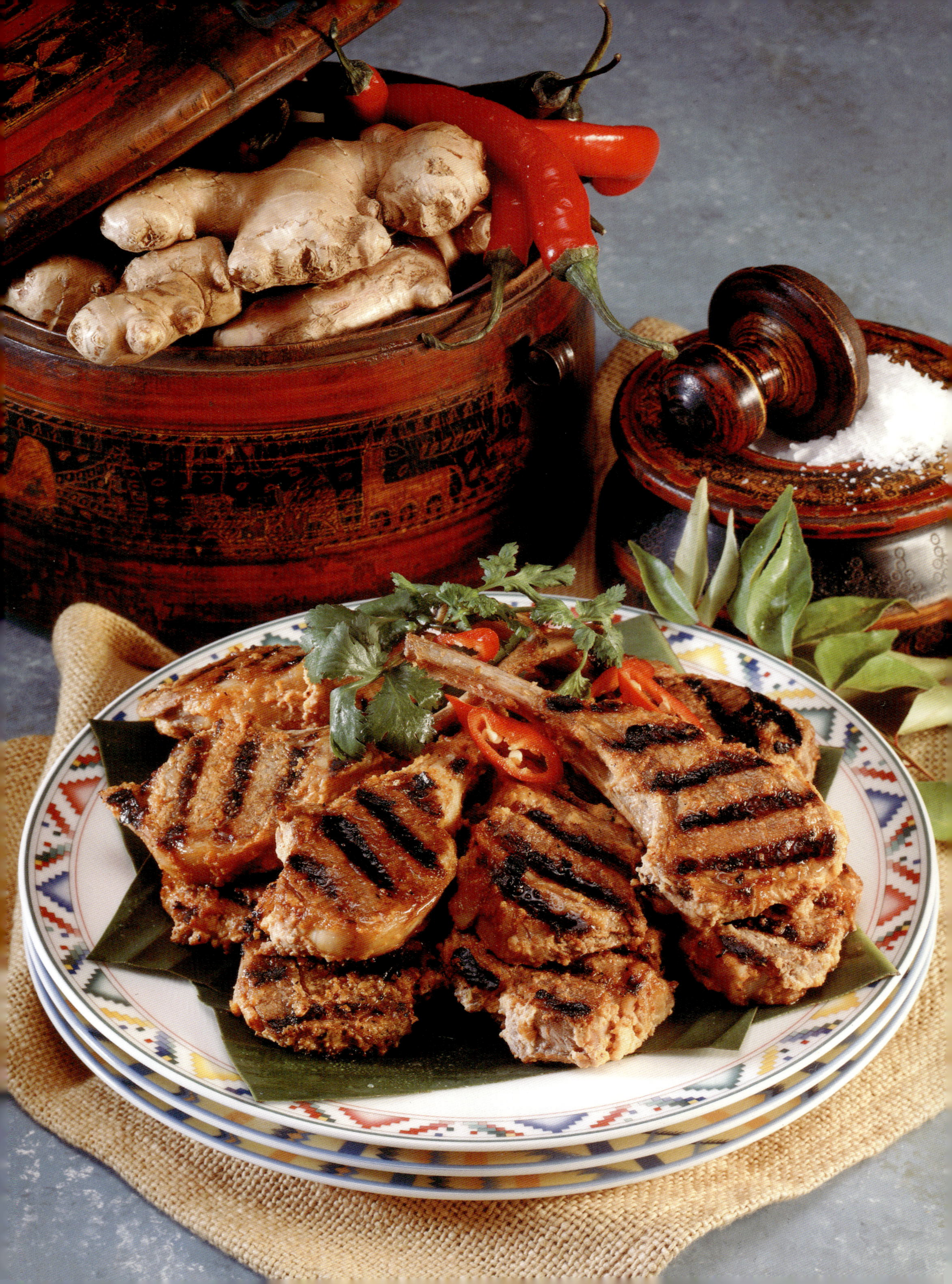

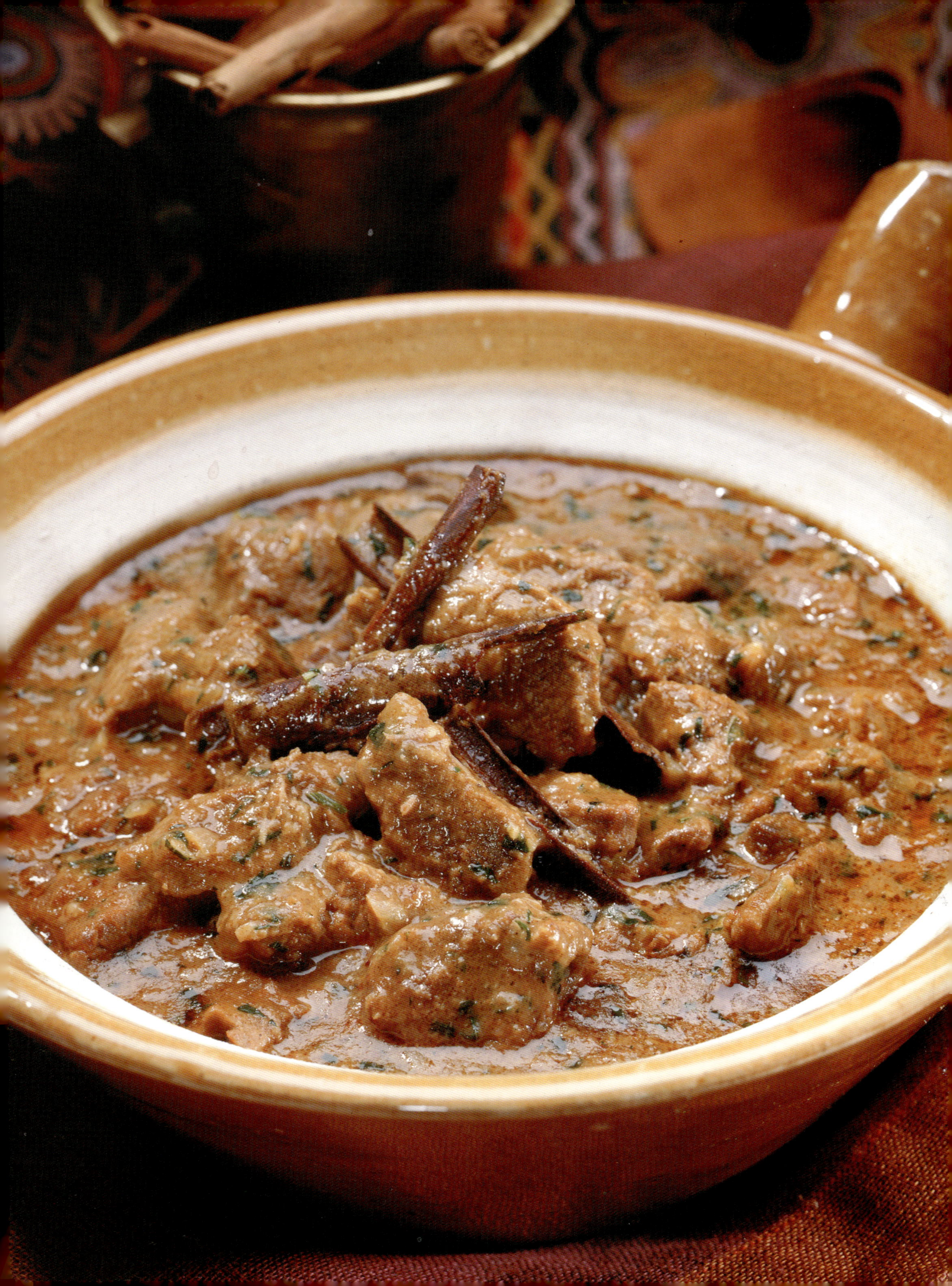

rogan josh

1 cup (250ml) yogurt
1 tablespoon malt vinegar
4 cloves garlic, crushed
1 tablespoon grated fresh ginger
1kg diced lamb
2 tablespoons ghee
4 cardamom pods, bruised
3 cloves
1 cinnamon stick
2 medium onions (300g), chopped finely
3 teaspoons ground cumin
1 tablespoon ground coriander
1 teaspoon ground fennel
1½ teaspoons sweet paprika
¾ teaspoon chilli powder
½ cup (125ml) chicken stock
1 teaspoon garam masala
2 tablespoons chopped fresh coriander
1 tablespoon chopped fresh mint

1. Combine yogurt, vinegar, half the garlic and half the ginger in large bowl, add lamb; toss lamb to coat in marinade. Cover; refrigerate 3 hours or overnight.
2. Heat ghee in large saucepan, add whole spices; cook, stirring, until fragrant. Add onions and remaining garlic and ginger; cook, stirring, until onions are browned lightly.
3. Add ground spices to pan; cook, stirring, until fragrant. Add lamb mixture, stir to coat in spice mixture.
4. Pour stock into pan; simmer, covered, 1½ hours. Simmer, uncovered, 30 minutes or until lamb is tender. Just before serving, stir in garam masala and fresh herbs.

serves 6 to 8

Toss lamb to coat in yogurt marinade; cover, refrigerate.

Cook onions, garlic and ginger with spices, until browned lightly.

Simmer, uncovered, 30 minutes or until lamb is tender.

MEAT

bandami lamb

1. Combine saffron and boiling water; stand 10 minutes.
2. Combine yogurt and undrained saffron in large bowl, add lamb; toss lamb to coat in marinade. Cover and refrigerate 1 hour.
3. Blend or process mint leaves, cold water and jaggery until pureed; reserve.
4. Heat ghee and oil in large saucepan; cook onions, stirring, until browned lightly. Add garlic, ginger and all spices; cook, stirring, until fragrant. Add lamb and mint mixtures to pan, stir well; simmer, covered, 1 hour.
5. Add nuts, juice and coriander and extra mint; simmer, uncovered, 10 minutes or until lamb is tender and mixture thickened. Serve topped with yogurt, if desired.

serves 6 to 8

¼ teaspoon saffron threads
¼ cup (60ml) boiling water
1 cup (250ml) yogurt
1.5kg diced lamb
½ cup firmly packed fresh mint leaves
¾ cup (180ml) cold water
25g jaggery
2 tablespoons ghee
1 tablespoon vegetable oil
2 medium onions (300g), sliced
4 cloves garlic, crushed
1 tablespoon grated fresh ginger
1 tablespoon ground cumin
1 cinnamon stick
6 cardamom pods, bruised
6 cloves
½ cup (60g) ground almonds
1 tablespoon lime juice
¼ cup chopped fresh coriander
2 tablespoons chopped fresh mint, extra

Combine saffron and boiling water; stand 10 minutes.

Blend or process mint, water and jaggery until pureed.

Simmer mixture until thickened and lamb is tender.

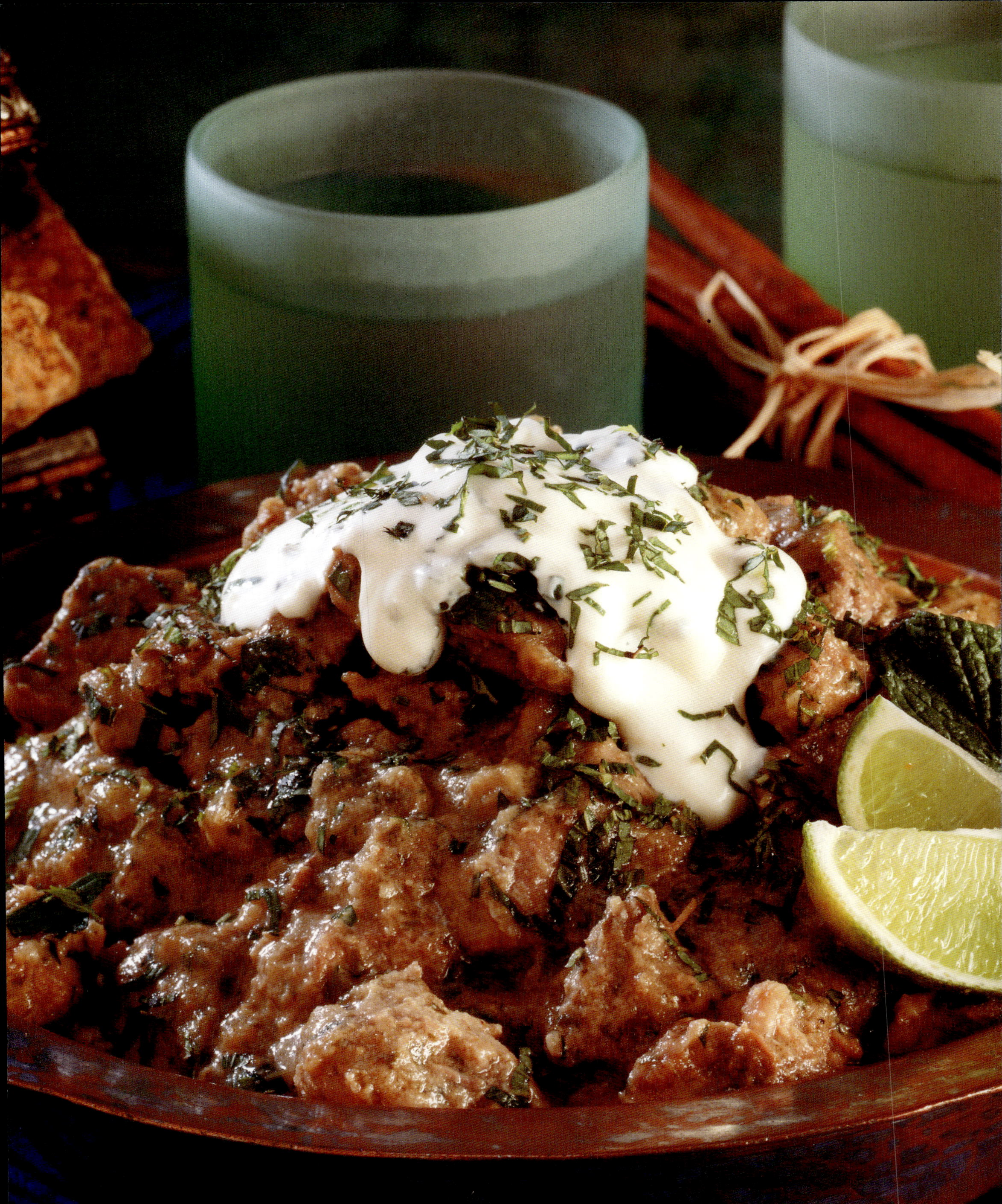

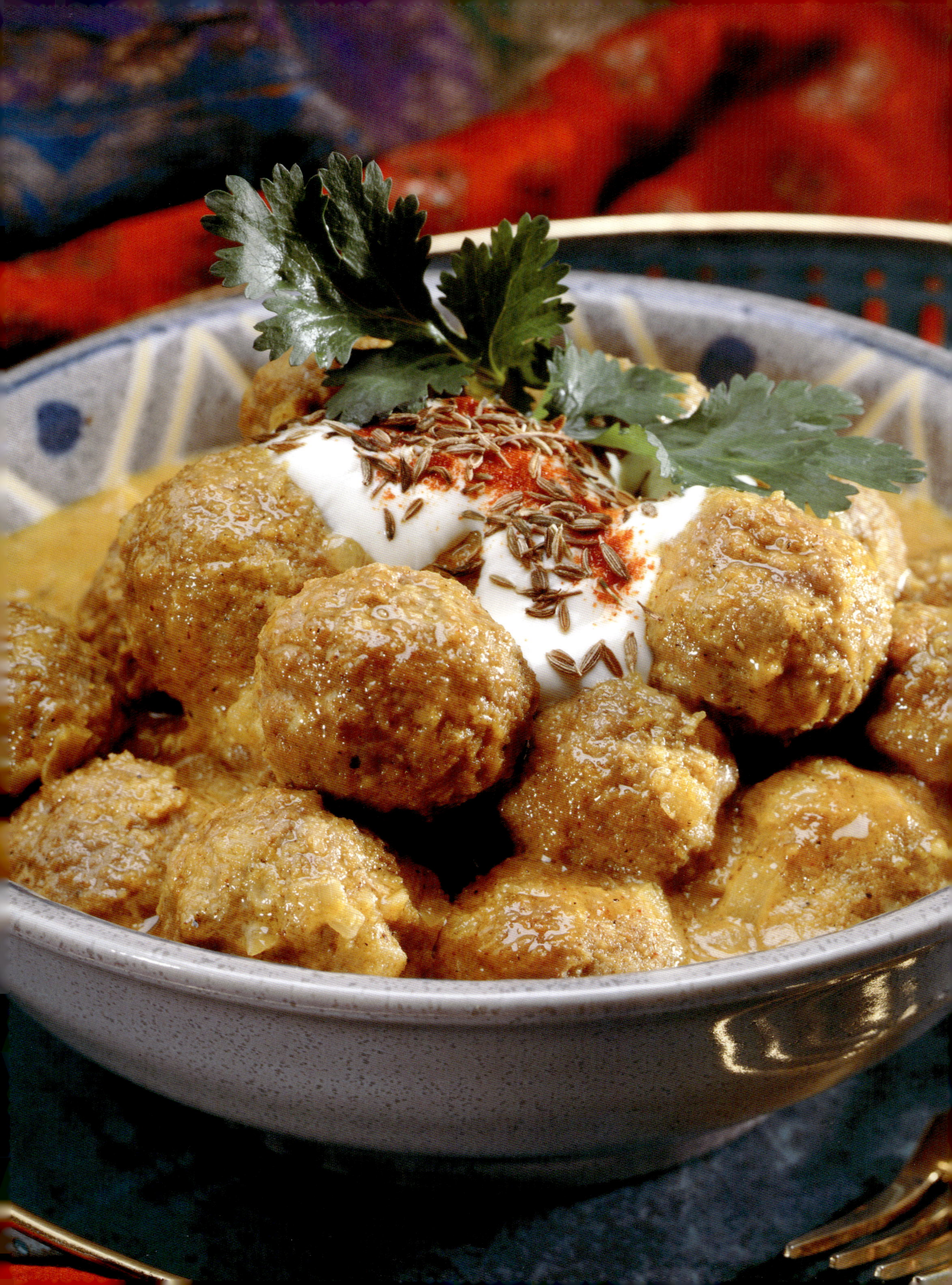

kashmiri lamb kofta

2 teaspoons ground cumin
2 teaspoons ground coriander
2 teaspoons garam masala
1 teaspoon chilli powder
½ teaspoon ground turmeric
750g minced lamb
4 cloves garlic, crushed
2 teaspoons grated fresh ginger
⅔ cup (160ml) yogurt
2 tablespoons ghee
1 large onion (200g), chopped
2 tablespoons full cream milk powder
2 tablespoons ground almonds
1 teaspoon sugar
1½ cups (375ml) hot water
⅓ cup (80ml) yogurt, extra

1. Combine spices in small bowl.
2. Combine the mince, garlic, ginger, 1 tablespoon of the yogurt and half of the spice mixture in large bowl; mix well. Using floured hands, roll tablespoons of spicy mince mixture into round kofta shapes.
3. Heat ghee in large saucepan; cook onion, stirring, until fragrant. Gradually add the remaining yogurt, milk powder, nuts, sugar and hot water. Bring to boil, then simmer, uncovered, 5 minutes, stirring occasionally, or until mixture thickens slightly.
4. Add kofta; simmer, covered, 10 minutes. Simmer, uncovered, 10 minutes or until kofta are cooked through and sauce is thickened. Serve topped with extra yogurt.

serves 6

Place all ground spices in small bowl; mix well.

Using floured hands, roll mince mixture into round kofta shapes.

Add kofta to yogurt mixture; simmer until cooked through.

punjabi lamb shanks in spinach and tomatoes

1 Blend or process garlic, chillies, ginger, cumin and oil until pureed. Spread chilli mixture all over lamb shanks; cover, refrigerate 3 hours or overnight.
2 Heat ghee in large saucepan; cook onions, stirring, until browned lightly. Add bay leaves and spices; cook, stirring, until fragrant. Add lamb mixture; cook, stirring, until lamb is just browned.
3 Boil, steam or microwave spinach until just wilted; drain. Blend or process spinach, undrained crushed tomatoes and paste until pureed; add to lamb mixture. Simmer, covered, for 1¼ hours. Simmer, uncovered, 30 minutes or until lamb is tender and sauce is thickened.

serves 4

4 cloves garlic
4 large green chillies
1 tablespoon grated fresh ginger
1 tablespoon ground cumin
2 tablespoons vegetable oil
8 french trimmed lamb shanks (1.5kg)
2 tablespoons ghee
2 medium onions (300g), sliced
2 bay leaves
4 cloves
1 cinnamon stick
1 cardamom pod, bruised
2 teaspoons garam masala
1 teaspoon ground nutmeg
1 teaspoon ground coriander
1 teaspoon ground cumin, extra
500g spinach, chopped
400g can tomatoes
¼ cup (60ml) tomato paste

Spread chilli mixture over lamb shanks; cover and refrigerate.

Add lamb to spices; cook, stirring, until just browned.

Simmer spinach mixture and lamb until tender and sauce thickens.

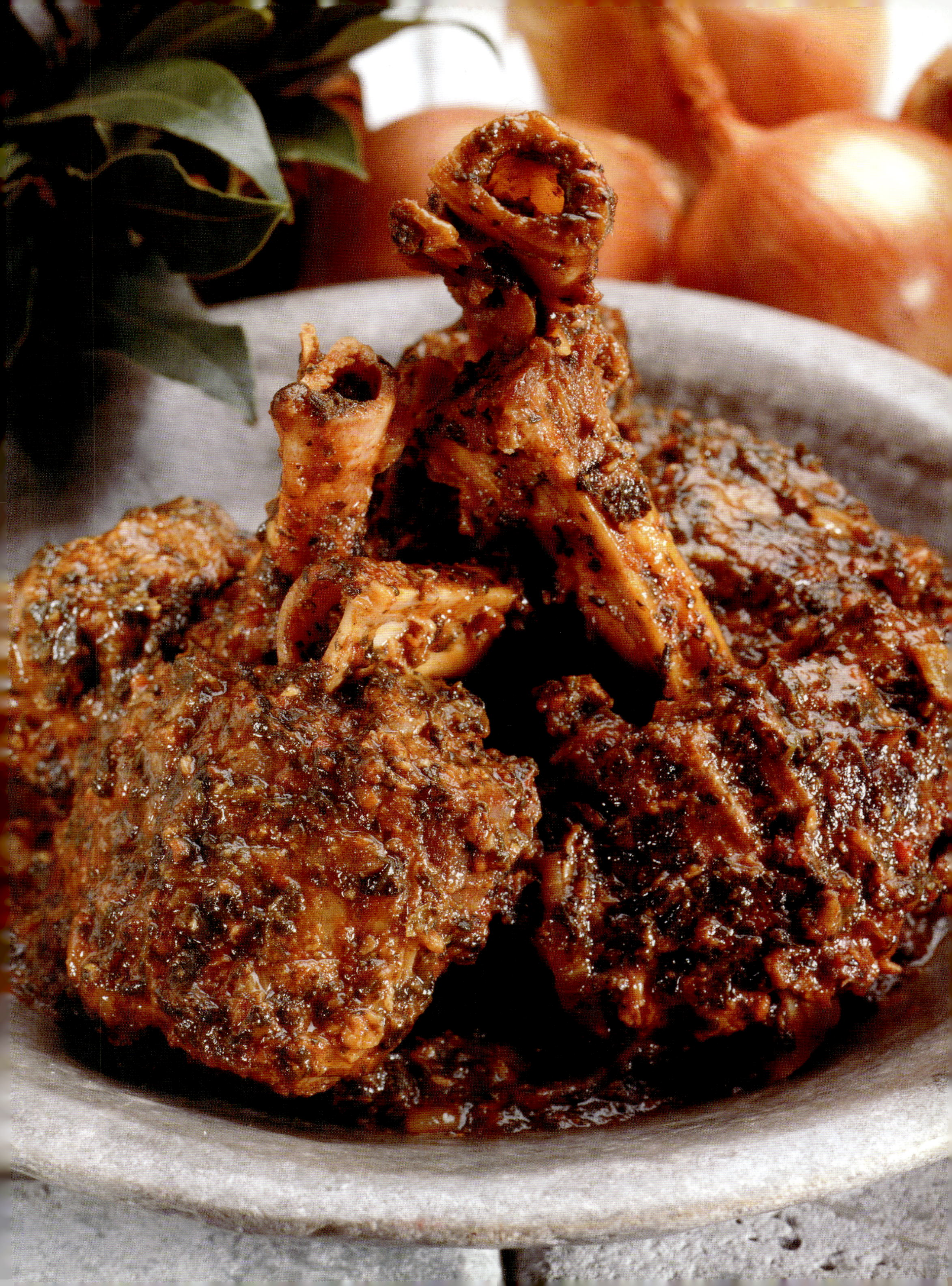

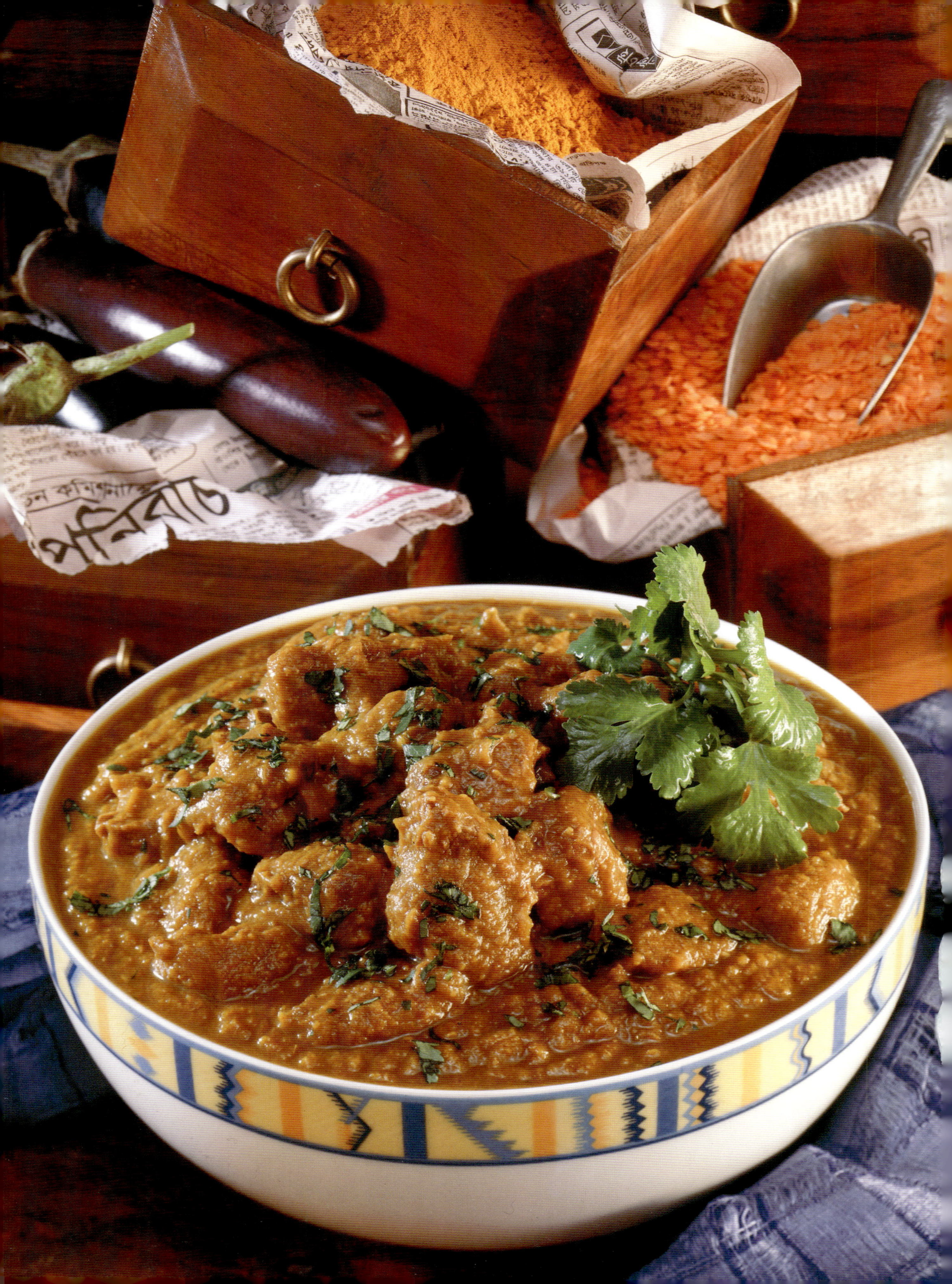

MEAT

beef dhansak

2 tablespoons ghee

2 medium onions (300g), chopped

4 cloves garlic, crushed

1 teaspoon ground turmeric

2 teaspoons ground coriander

2 teaspoons ground cumin

2 teaspoons garam masala

500g pumpkin, peeled, chopped

1 medium eggplant (300g), peeled, chopped

6 curry leaves

1 cup (200g) masoor dhal (red lentils), rinsed, drained

1 litre (4 cups) water

1kg diced beef

1 Heat ghee in large saucepan; cook onions and garlic, stirring, until browned lightly. Add all the spices; cook, stirring, until fragrant.
2 Add pumpkin to pan along with eggplant, curry leaves, dhal and water; bring to the boil, then immediately simmer. Cook, covered, 30 minutes or until pumpkin is tender. Cool.
3 Blend or process mixture, in batches, until pureed; return to same pan.
4 Add diced beef to pan; bring to the boil, then immediately simmer. Cook, covered, 1 hour. Simmer, uncovered, 30 minutes or until beef is tender and mixture thickened.

serves 6

Cook spices in onion mixture, stirring, until fragrant.

Process pumpkin and dhal mixture, in batches, until pureed.

MEAT

lamb do piaza

1. Finely slice half the onions. Heat half the ghee in large saucepan; cook sliced onions until browned lightly. Remove from pan; reserve.
2. Finely chop remaining onions. Heat remaining ghee in same pan, add onions, garlic and ginger; cook, stirring, until onions are browned lightly. Stir in chilli powder and all spices; cook, stirring, until fragrant.
3. Stir lamb into spice mixture; add yogurt gradually, in six batches, stirring well between additions.
4. Add undrained crushed tomatoes; simmer, covered, 1½ hours. Remove cover; simmer 30 minutes or until lamb is tender.
5. Just before serving, add reserved onions, herbs and garam masala; stir until heated through.

serves 6 to 8

4 large onions (800g)
3 tablespoons ghee
5 cloves garlic, crushed
1 tablespoon grated fresh ginger
½ teaspoon chilli powder
½ teaspoon ground coriander
1 tablespoon ground cumin
1 teaspoon ground turmeric
½ teaspoon cardamom seeds
4 cloves
1.2kg diced lamb
1 cup (250ml) yogurt
400g can tomatoes
2 tablespoons chopped fresh coriander
2 tablespoons chopped fresh mint
1½ teaspoons garam masala

Stir powder and spices into chopped onion mixture until fragrant.

Add tomatoes to lamb mixture; simmer until lamb is tender.

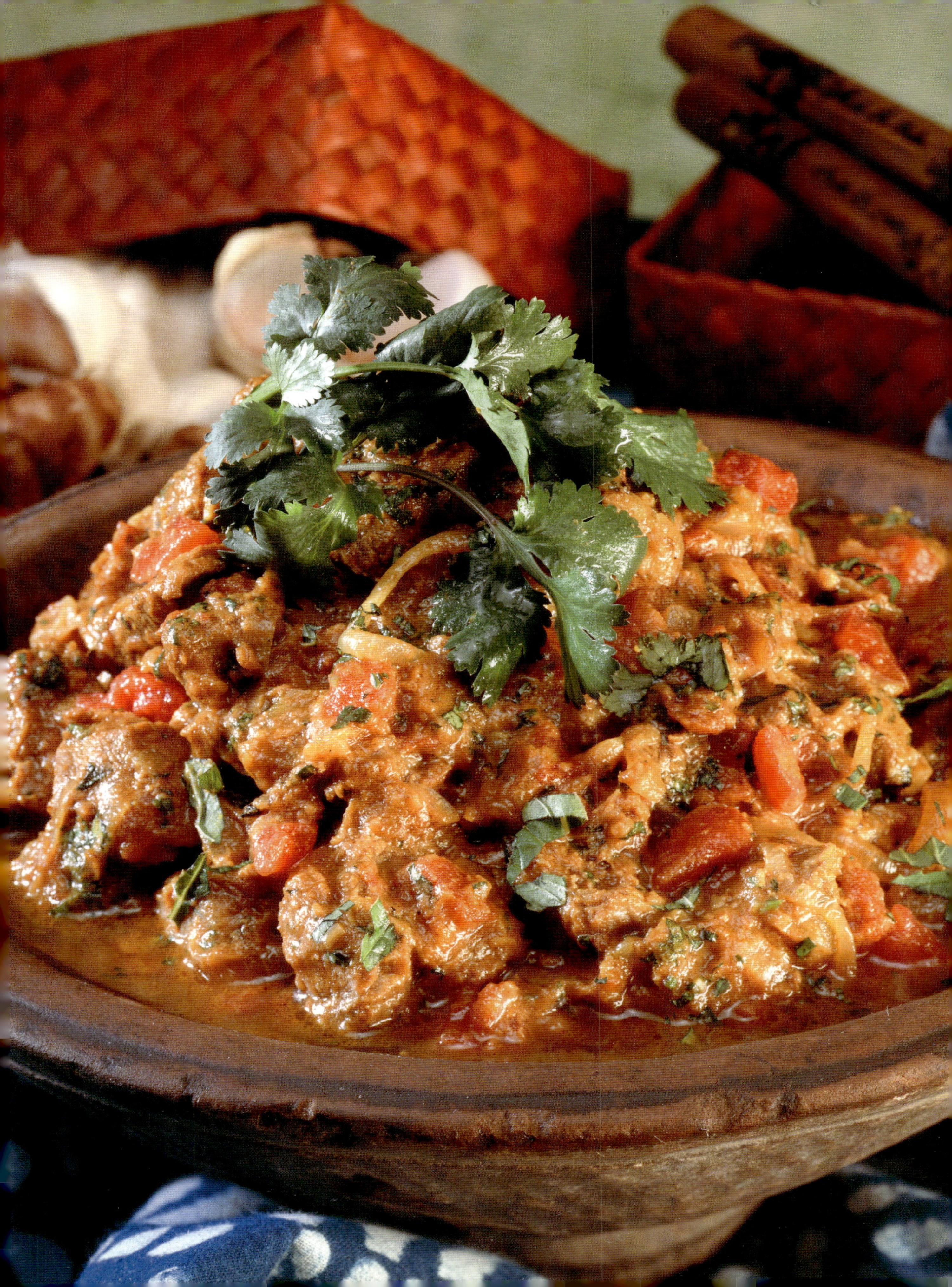

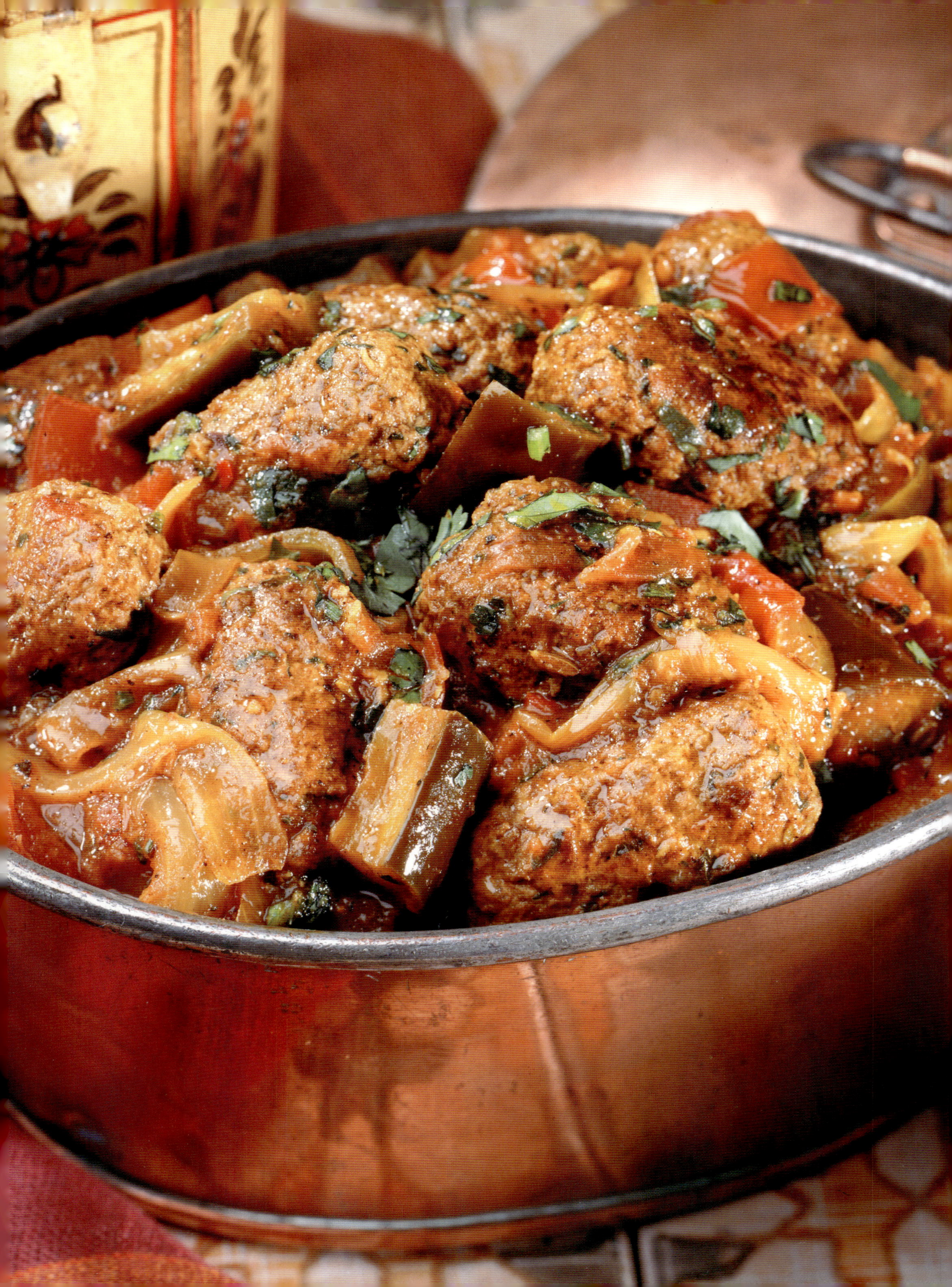

beef kofta with eggplant and tomato masala

750g minced beef

2 tablespoons chopped fresh mint

2 teaspoons finely grated fresh ginger

1 teaspoon ground coriander

½ teaspoon garam masala

1 teaspoon chilli powder

¼ cup (60ml) yogurt

3 tablespoons ghee

2 medium onions (300g), sliced

2 cloves garlic, crushed

½ teaspoon ground cardamom

1 teaspoon garam masala, extra

1 teaspoon ground turmeric

1 teaspoon cumin seeds

2 medium tomatoes (380g), chopped

1 tablespoon tomato paste

2 baby eggplants (120g), chopped

2 small red chillies, chopped finely

1 cup (250ml) beef stock

1 tablespoon chopped fresh coriander

1 Combine mince, mint, ginger, ground coriander, garam masala, chilli powder and yogurt in medium bowl. Mould tablespoons of mince mixture into oval kofta shapes, place on tray; cover, refrigerate 1 hour.
2 Heat half the ghee in large frying pan; cook kofta, in batches, until browned all over. Drain on absorbent paper.
3 Heat remaining ghee in same pan; cook onions, garlic, cardamom, extra garam masala, turmeric and cumin, stirring, until onions are browned lightly.
4 Add tomatoes, paste, eggplants and chillies; cook, stirring, 5 minutes or until vegetables are soft.
5 Add stock and kofta; simmer, covered, 20 minutes. Simmer, uncovered, 10 minutes or until kofta are cooked through and sauce is thickened. Just before serving, stir in chopped fresh coriander.

serves 6 to 8

Mould mince mixture into oval kofta shapes; refrigerate.

Add tomatoes, paste, eggplants and chillies; cook until soft.

lamb korma

1. Heat 1 tablespoon oil in large saucepan; cook chillies, nuts and onions, stirring, until onions are browned lightly. Cool.
2. Blend or process onion mixture with half the blended coconut milk powder and water.
3. Heat remaining oil in same pan; cook garlic, ginger and spices, stirring, until fragrant. Stir diced lamb into spice mixture; add yogurt gradually, in batches, stirring well between additions.
4. Add onion mixture to pan along with remaining coconut milk mixture and undrained crushed tomatoes; simmer, covered, 1 hour. Simmer, uncovered, 1 hour or until lamb is tender. Just before serving, stir in tamarind.

serves 8

2 tablespoons vegetable oil
2 small green chillies, chopped
½ cup (75g) raw cashews
2 medium onions (300g), chopped roughly
¾ cup (100g) coconut milk powder
¾ cup (180ml) boiling water
3 cloves garlic, crushed
1½ tablespoons grated fresh ginger
1 tablespoon ground cumin
3 teaspoons ground coriander
1½ teaspoons garam masala
6 cardamom pods, bruised
1 cinnamon stick
2 cloves
1.5kg diced lamb
⅔ cup (160ml) yogurt
400g can tomatoes
1 tablespoon tamarind concentrate

Blend onion mixture with half the blended milk powder and water.

Cook garlic, ginger and spices, stirring, until fragrant.

Stir yogurt, in batches, into spicy lamb mixture.

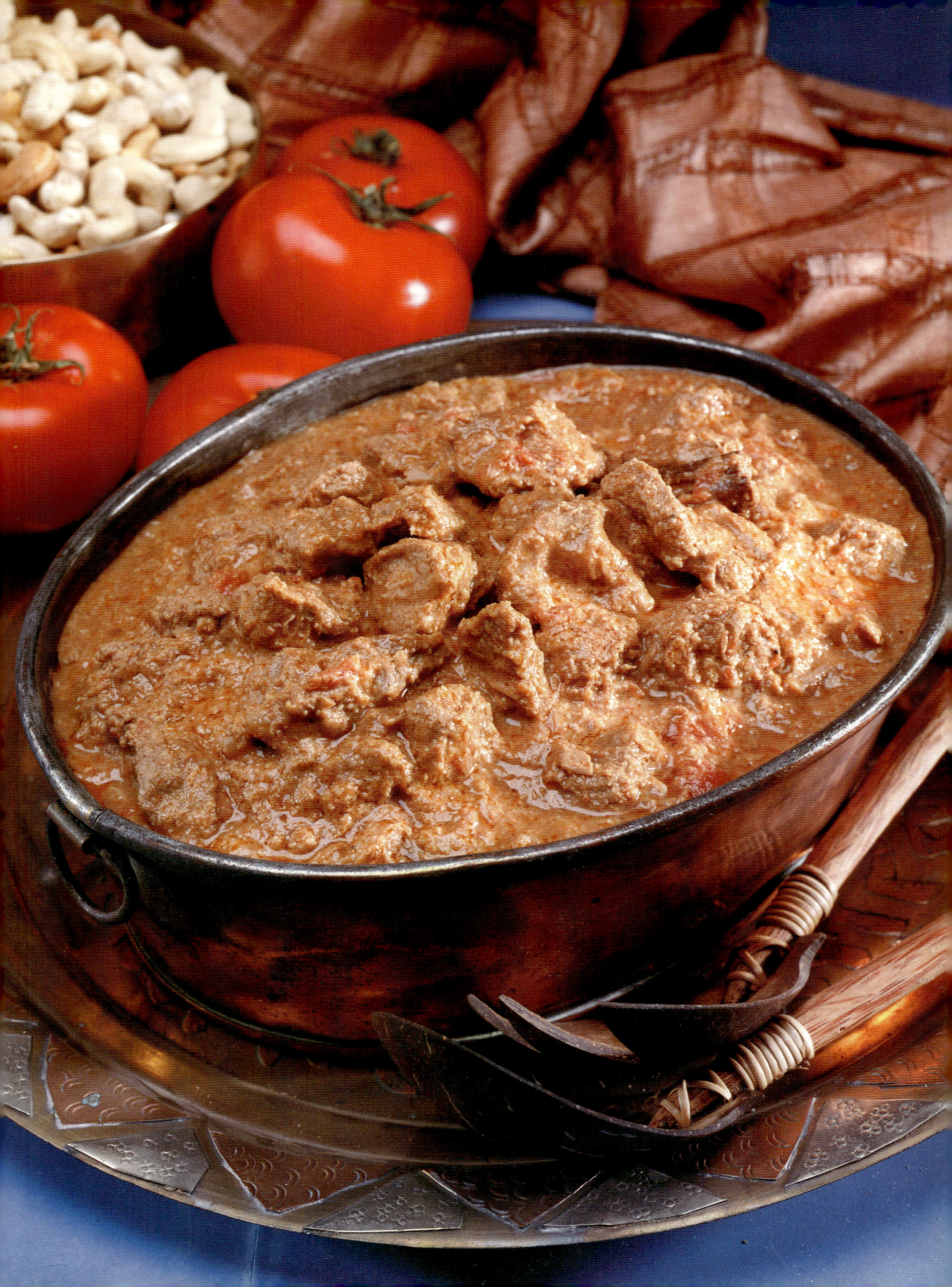

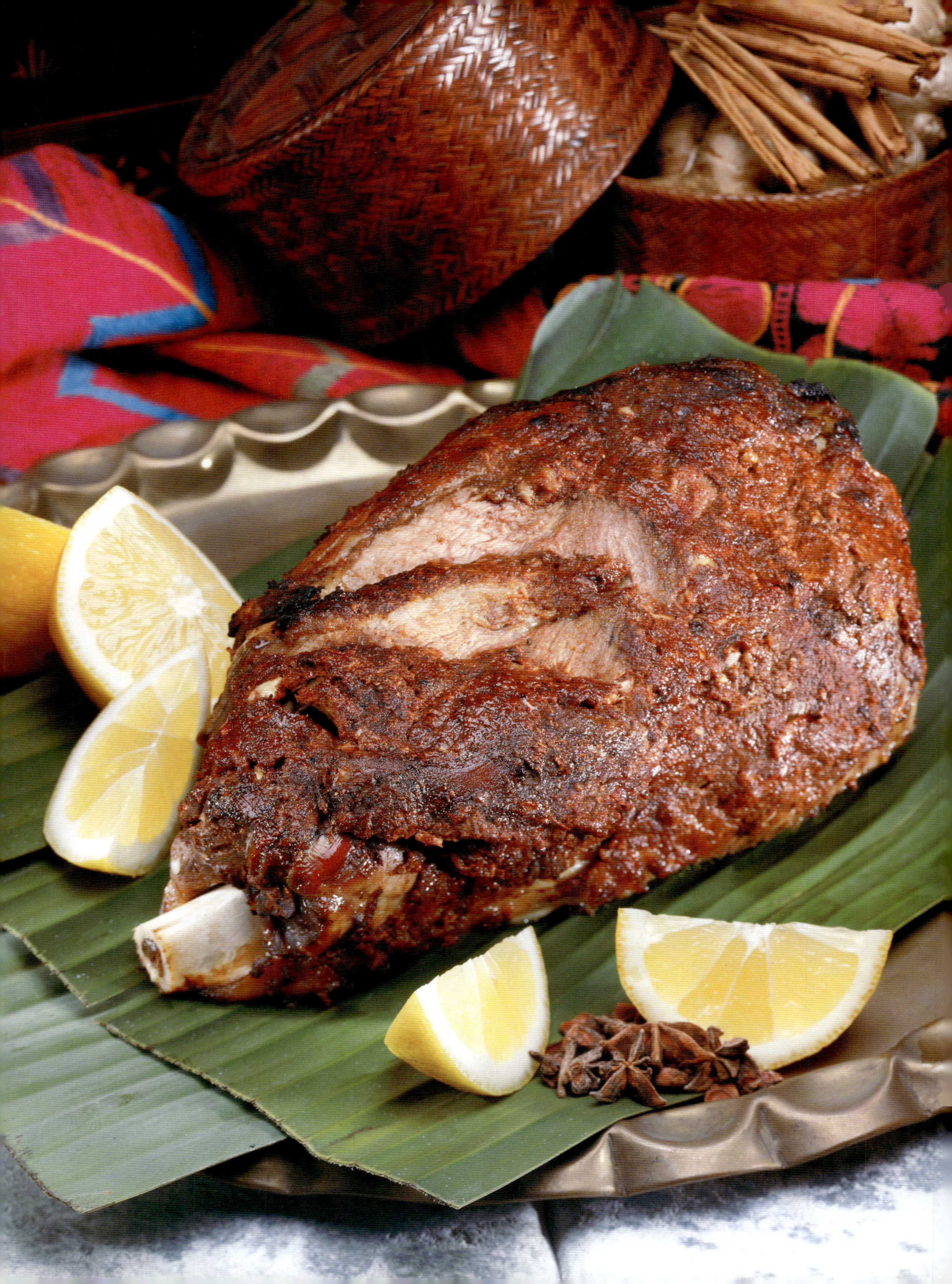

raan

2 teaspoons coriander seeds
1 teaspoon cumin seeds
8 cardamom pods, bruised
2 cinnamon sticks, crushed
2 star anise
½ teaspoon black pepper
6 cloves
4 cloves garlic, crushed
1 tablespoon grated fresh ginger
2 tablespoons lemon juice
¼ cup (60ml) tomato paste
2kg leg of lamb
½ cup (125ml) boiling water
¼ teaspoon saffron threads

1 Combine seeds and spices in dry hot frying pan; cook, stirring, until fragrant.
2 Grind or process the cooled spice mixture until crushed. Combine spice mixture, garlic, ginger, juice and paste in small bowl; mix well.
3 Trim fat from lamb; pierce lamb all over, making deep cuts with the tip of a sharp knife. Rub spice mixture over lamb, pressing firmly into the cuts. Place lamb in large bowl; cover, refrigerate at least 24 hours.
4 Preheat oven to moderate.
5 Pour combined water and saffron into large baking dish; place lamb on oven rack in dish. Cover with foil; bake in moderate oven 1 hour or until lamb is tender. Remove and discard foil; bake 30 minutes or until lamb is well browned.

serves 6 to 8

Combine spice mixture, garlic, ginger, juice and paste in a bowl.

Pierce lamb all over, making deep cuts with a knife.

Place spice-rubbed lamb on rack in large baking dish.

pork vindaloo

1. Cook cumin and garam masala in large dry saucepan, stirring, until fragrant.
2. Combine cooled spice mixture with ginger, garlic, chillies, vinegar and tamarind in large bowl, add pork; toss pork to coat in marinade. Cover; refrigerate 1 hour.
3. Heat ghee in same pan; cook onions, cinnamon and cloves, stirring, until onions are browned lightly. Add pork mixture; cook, stirring, 5 minutes or until pork is browned lightly. Stir in flour.
4. Gradually pour in stock, then stir in leaves; simmer, covered, 30 minutes. Simmer, uncovered, 30 minutes or until pork is tender and sauce thickened. Add jaggery; stir until dissolved.

serves 6 to 8

- 2 teaspoons cumin seeds
- 2 teaspoons garam masala
- 1 tablespoon grated fresh ginger
- 6 cloves garlic, crushed
- 8 small red chillies, chopped finely
- 1 tablespoon white vinegar
- 1 tablespoon tamarind concentrate
- 1kg diced pork
- 2 tablespoons ghee
- 2 large onions (400g), chopped
- 2 cinnamon sticks
- 6 cloves
- 2 teaspoons plain flour
- 1 litre (4 cups) beef stock
- 8 curry leaves
- 25g jaggery

Combine marinade ingredients and pork in large bowl; refrigerate.

Cook pork mixture until browned lightly; stir in flour.

Simmer vindaloo until pork is tender and sauce thickened.

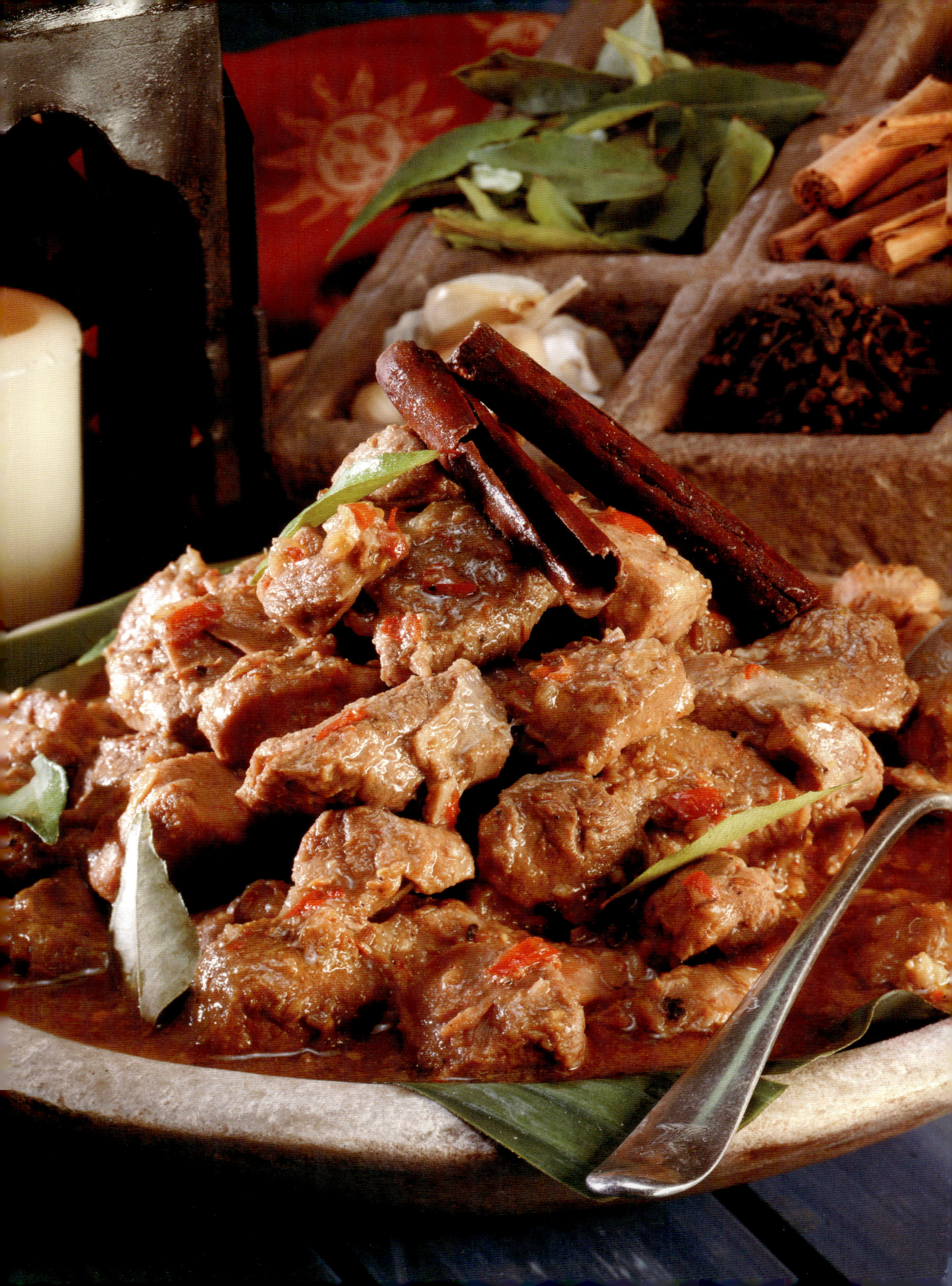

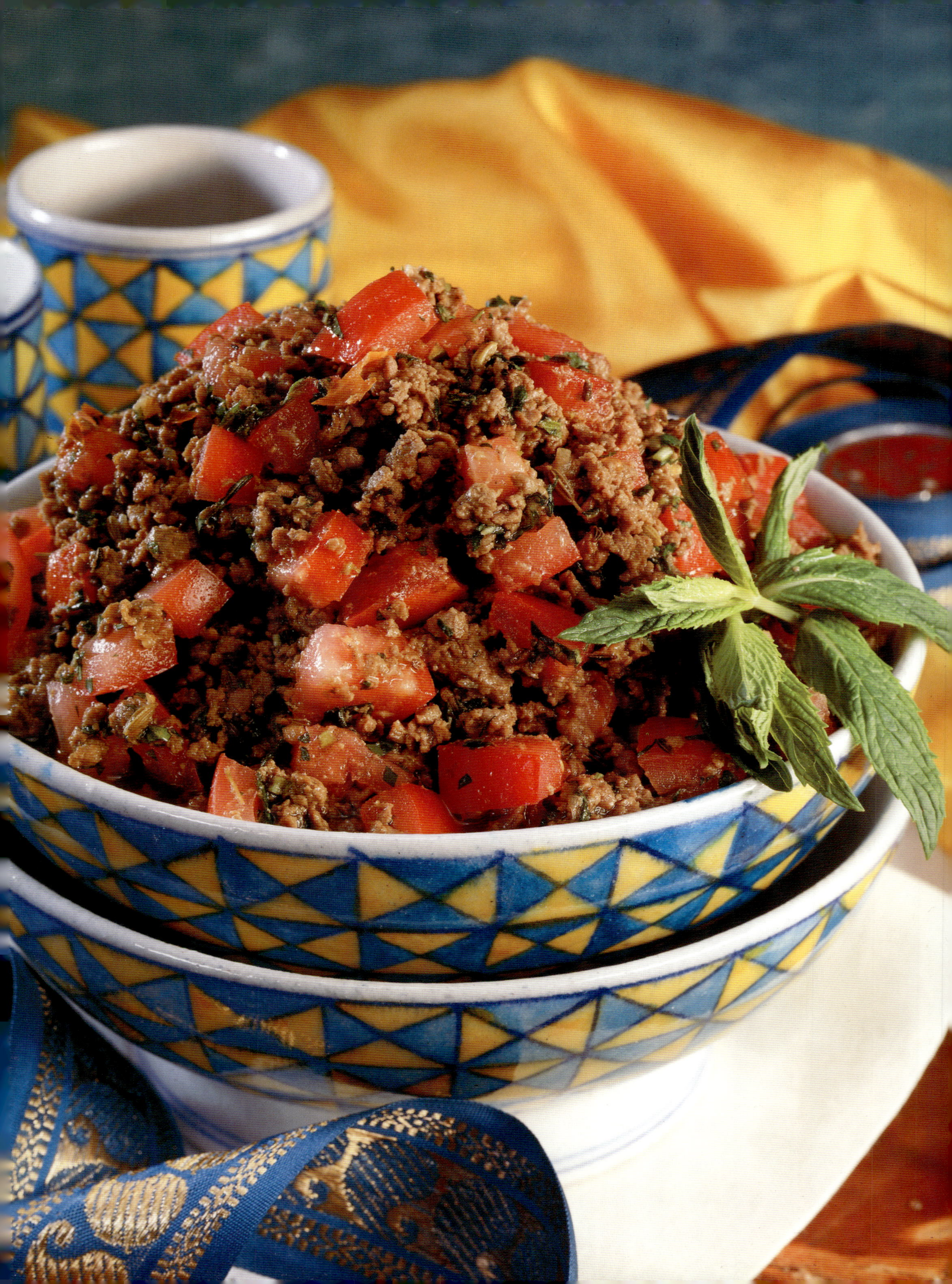

lamb kheema

- 2 tablespoons ghee
- 2 medium onions (300g), sliced
- 2 cloves garlic, crushed
- 1 tablespoon grated fresh ginger
- 3 large dried red chillies, crushed
- 1 tablespoon fennel seeds
- 2 teaspoons cumin seeds
- 1 teaspoon ground turmeric
- 1 teaspoon ground cardamom
- 3 bay leaves
- 1kg minced lamb
- 1 cup (250ml) chicken stock
- 2 medium tomatoes (380g), chopped
- ½ cup chopped fresh mint

1. Heat ghee in large saucepan; cook onions, stirring, until browned. Add garlic, ginger, chillies, seeds, spices and bay leaves to pan; cook, stirring, until fragrant.
2. Add mince to pan; cook, stirring, until well browned. Pour in stock; bring to boil, then immediately simmer. Cook, covered, 30 minutes. Cook, uncovered, stirring occasionally, until all liquid has evaporated. Discard bay leaves.
3. Just before serving, add tomatoes and mint to pan; stir until heated through.

serves 6 to 8

Cook garlic, ginger, chillies, seeds, spices and leaves until fragrant.

Add mince to pan; cook, stirring, until well browned.

moglai leg of lamb

1 Heat ghee in large saucepan; cook onions, garlic, ginger, seeds and nuts, stirring, until onions are browned lightly.
2 Stir paste into onion spice mixture until well combined. Stir in combined stock and yogurt; add lamb, cinnamon and cardamom. Bring to the boil, then immediately simmer. Cook, covered, 1½ hours, turning occasionally, or until lamb is tender. Remove lamb; cover with foil to keep warm.
3 Bring sauce to the boil, then immediately simmer, uncovered, 10 minutes or until sauce is thickened. Serve lamb with sauce, sprinkled with fresh coriander.

serves 6 to 8

3 tablespoons ghee
2 medium onions (300g), sliced
4 cloves garlic, crushed
2 teaspoons finely grated fresh ginger
2 teaspoons cumin seeds
2 tablespoons ground almonds
⅓ cup (80ml) Madras curry paste
2 cups (500ml) beef stock
1¼ cups (310ml) yogurt
2kg leg of lamb
1 cinnamon stick
4 cardamom pods
¼ cup chopped fresh coriander

Simmer lamb and spices in curry mixture until lamb is tender.

Bring sauce to the boil; simmer 10 minutes until thickened.

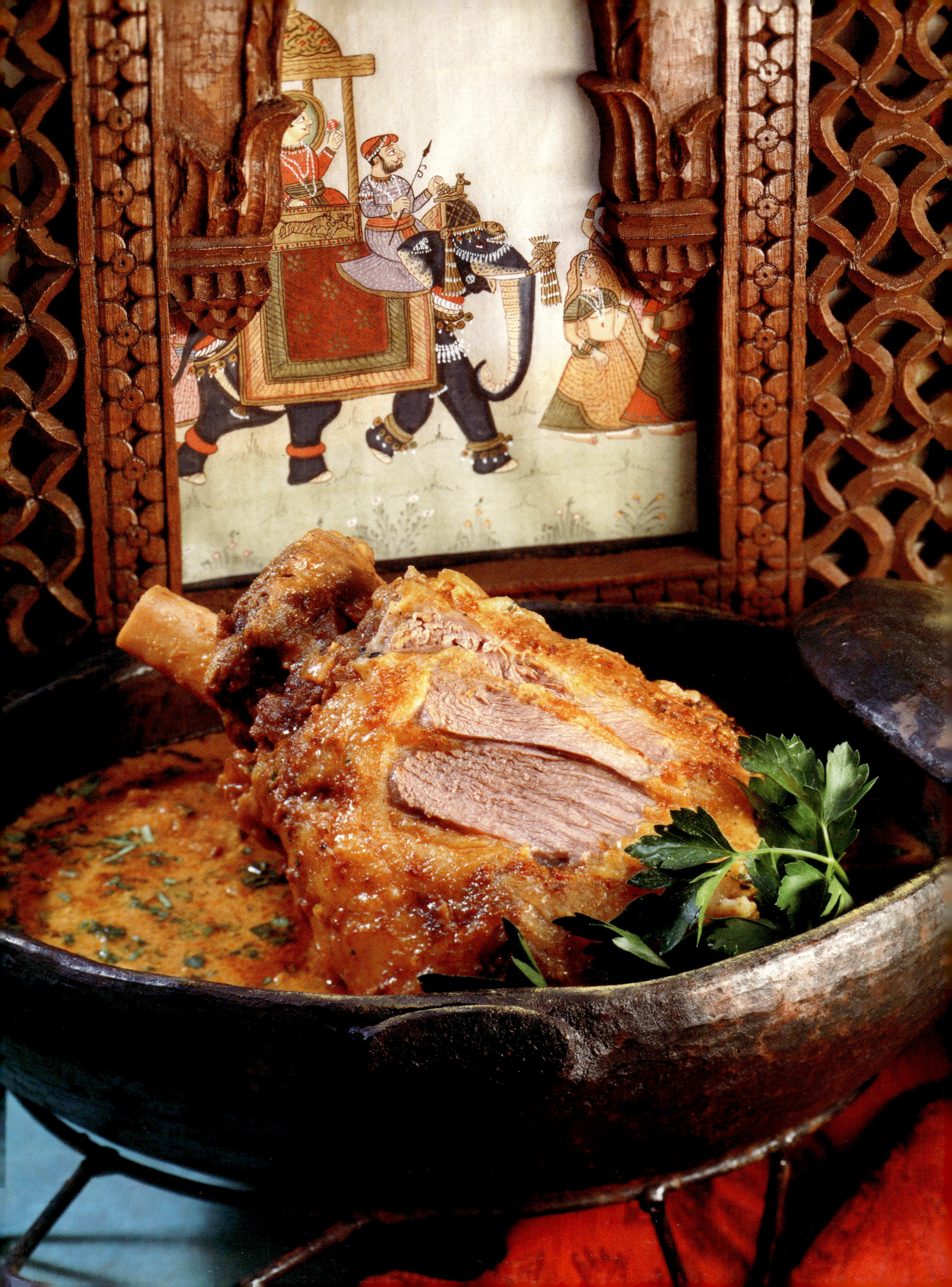

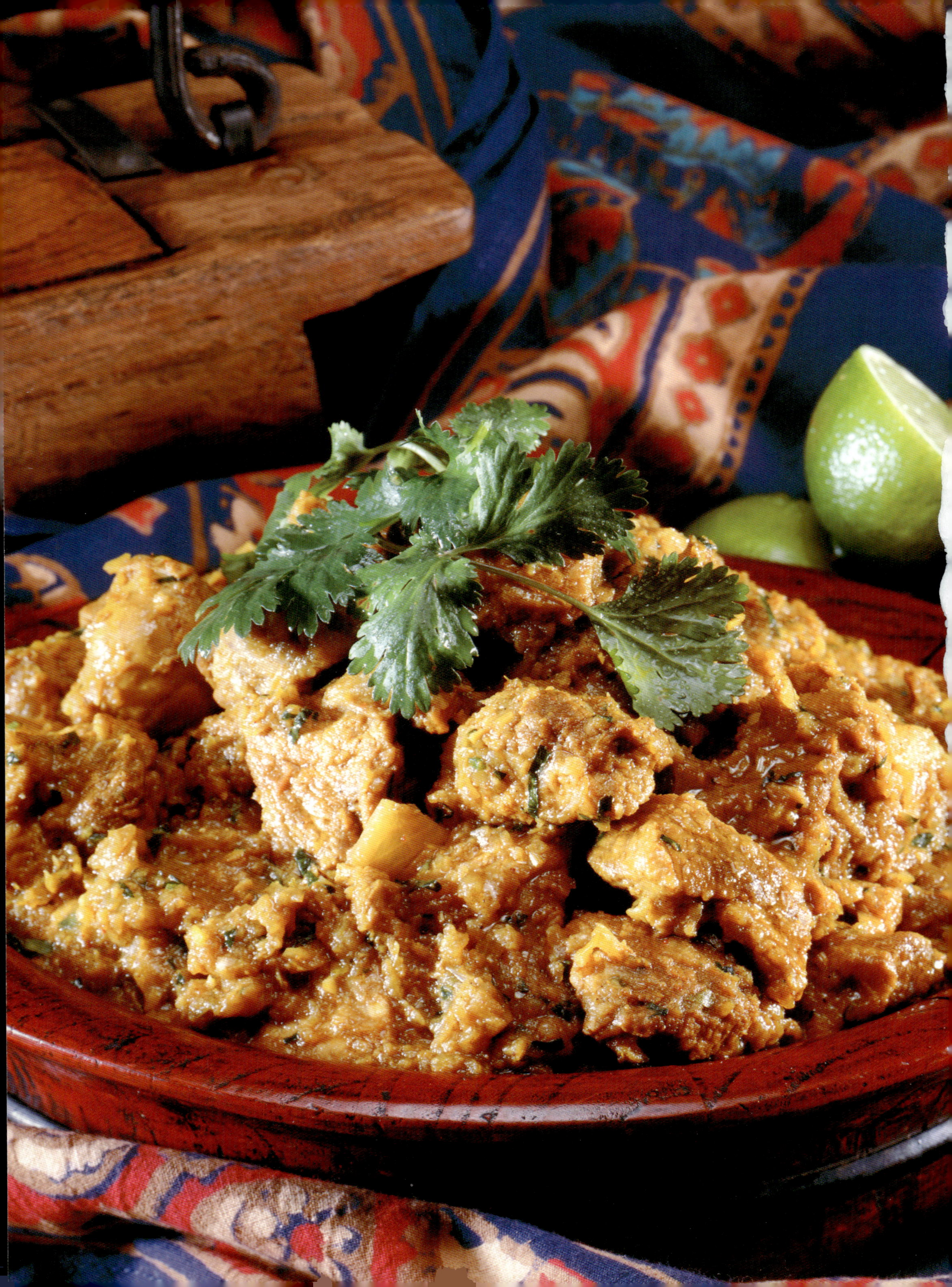

MEAT

pork and tamarind curry

60g dried tamarind, chopped
2 cups (500ml) boiling water
1 large onion (200g), chopped
4 cloves garlic
1 teaspoon finely grated fresh ginger
2 small green chillies
1 tablespoon chopped lemon grass
2 tablespoons ghee
5 cloves
2 cinnamon sticks
1 teaspoon ground turmeric
1 tablespoon ground coriander
½ teaspoon ground cardamom
1 teaspoon chilli powder
1kg diced pork
1 tablespoon chopped fresh coriander

1 Combine tamarind and boiling water in small bowl; stand 30 minutes. Strain tamarind over bowl, pressing to extract all liquid; discard tamarind. Reserve liquid.
2 Blend or process onion, garlic, ginger, chillies, lemon grass and 1 tablespoon reserved tamarind liquid until pureed.
3 Heat ghee in large saucepan; cook onion mixture, cloves, cinnamon and spices, stirring, until onion is soft and mixture fragrant. Add pork; cook, stirring, until pork is coated in spice mixture and changes colour.
4 Stir in remaining reserved tamarind liquid; simmer, covered, 30 minutes. Simmer, uncovered, 30 minutes or until pork is cooked through and tender. Just before serving, stir in chopped fresh coriander.

serves 6

Process onion, garlic, ginger, chillies, lemon grass and tamarind.

Cook pork in spice mixture until it changes colour.

Simmer curry until pork is cooked through and tender.

beef madras

1. Blend or process coconut, undrained tomatoes, ginger, seeds and tamarind until pureed.
2. Heat oil in large saucepan; cook onions and garlic, stirring, until browned lightly. Add all the spices; cook, stirring, until fragrant.
3. Add curry leaves, beef, water and pureed coconut mixture; simmer, covered, 1½ hours, stirring occasionally, or until beef is tender.

serves 6

1 cup (90g) grated fresh coconut
400g can tomatoes
2 tablespoons grated fresh ginger
2 teaspoons black mustard seeds
1 tablespoon tamarind concentrate
2 tablespoons vegetable oil
2 large onions (400g), sliced
6 cloves garlic, crushed
1 tablespoon ground cumin
1 teaspoon ground turmeric
2 teaspoons ground coriander
2 teaspoons hot chilli powder
2 teaspoons sweet paprika
10 curry leaves
1kg diced beef chuck steak
½ cup (125ml) water

Process coconut, tomatoes, ginger, seeds and tamarind.

Cook onion mixture and spices in pan until fragrant.

Simmer curry for 1½ hours or until beef is tender.

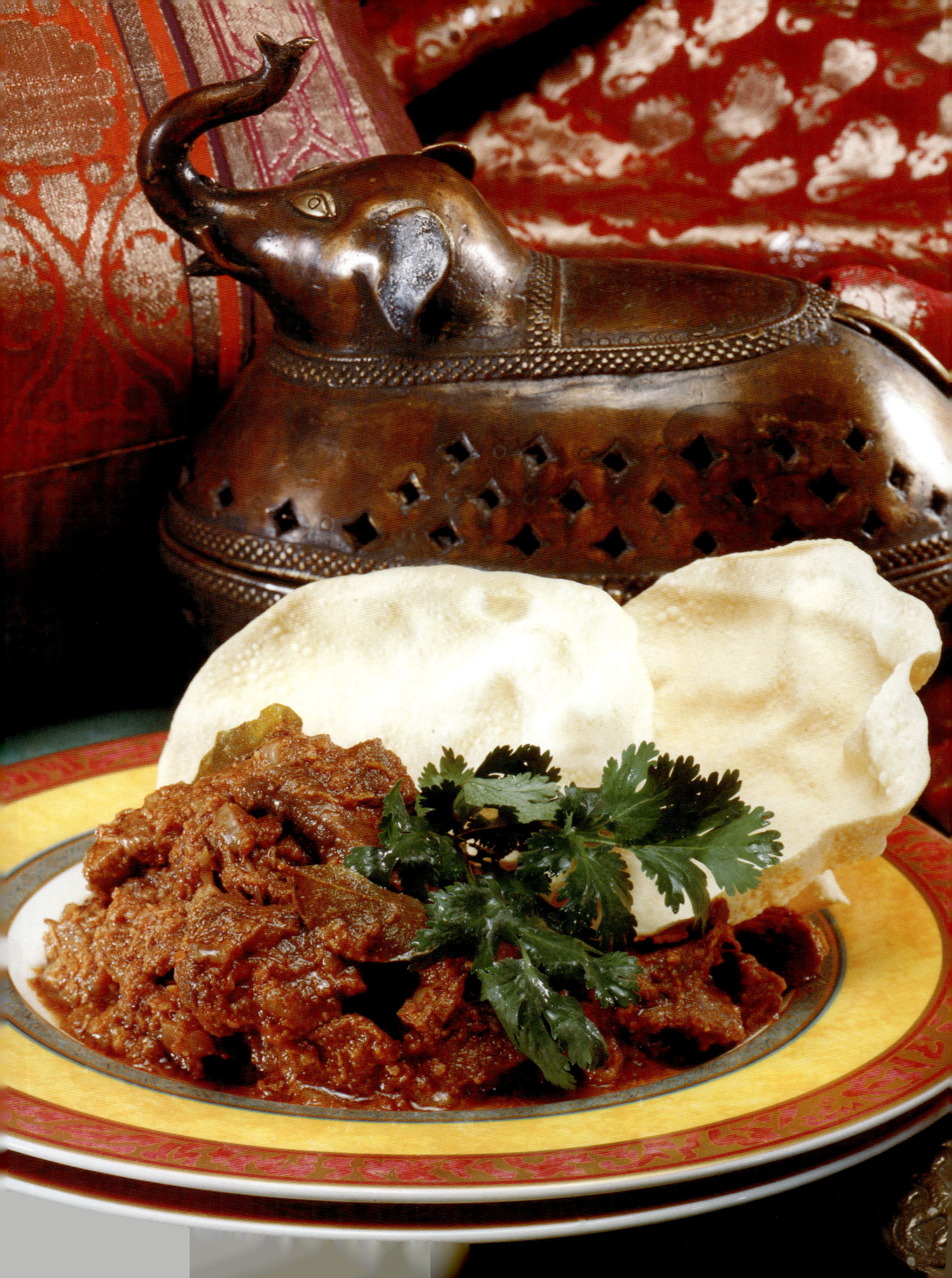

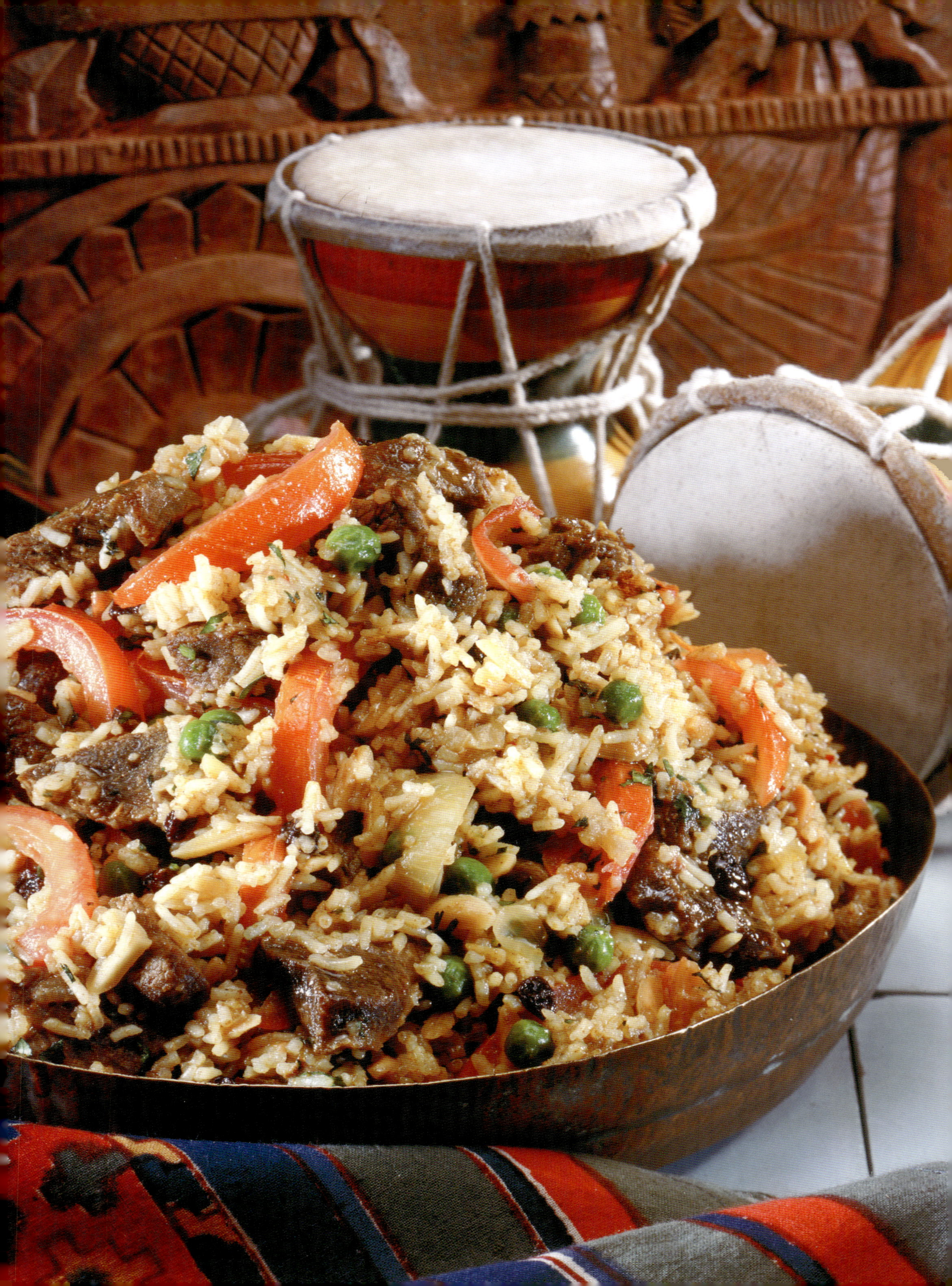

beef biryani

2 small red chillies, chopped finely
2 teaspoons ground coriander
2 teaspoons ground cumin
½ teaspoon ground turmeric
2 tablespoons white vinegar
⅓ cup (80ml) yogurt
1kg beef chuck steak, chopped
2 tablespoons ghee
2 large onions (400g), sliced
2 cinnamon sticks
4 cardamom pods, bruised
2 cups (400g) basmati rice
2¼ cups (560ml) beef stock
1½ cups (185g) frozen peas
⅓ cup (50g) currants
2 large tomatoes (500g), quartered, seeded, sliced
1 cup (140g) slivered almonds, toasted
¼ cup chopped fresh coriander

1 Combine chillies, ground spices, vinegar and yogurt in medium bowl, add beef; toss beef to coat in marinade. Cover; refrigerate 1 hour.
2 Heat ghee in large saucepan; cook onions, cinnamon and cardamom, stirring, until onions are browned lightly. Add beef mixture; simmer, covered, stirring occasionally, 1 hour or until beef is tender.
3 Meanwhile, place rice in medium bowl, cover with water; stand 30 minutes. Drain well.
4 Stir rice and stock into beef mixture; boil, then immediately simmer, covered, 10 minutes, stirring occasionally, or until rice is just tender. Discard cinnamon sticks. Stir in peas, currants and tomatoes; stand, covered, 10 minutes. Just before serving, stir in nuts and fresh coriander.

serves 4 to 6

Toss beef in yogurt marinade; refrigerate 1 hour.

Add beef mixture to onion mixture; simmer until beef is tender.

Stir in rice and stock; simmer until rice is tender.

RELISHES

Chutneys, pickles, sambals and raitas fulfil an important purpose on the Indian menu. Some of them provide the meal's only raw salad ingredient, others help temper the heat of a main-course curry... plus they're so delicious that some can even be eaten on their own, with naan or roti.

banana and coconut sambal

2 firm bananas, sliced
1 tablespoon lemon juice
1 teaspoon sugar
¼ teaspoon salt
1 small red chilli, chopped finely
¼ cup (20g) shredded coconut

Combine all ingredients in medium bowl; stir until well combined. Serve immediately.
makes about 2 cups

tomato and mint kachumber

4 medium tomatoes (760g)
1 medium onion (150g), sliced
¼ cup shredded fresh mint
¼ cup (60ml) lemon juice
2 teaspoons sugar
1 teaspoon salt

Peel and quarter tomatoes; discard seeds, then cut tomatoes into thin slices. Combine tomatoes, onion and mint in large bowl. Whisk juice, sugar and salt together in small, bowl then mix into tomato mixture. Cover; refrigerate at least 30 minutes.
serves 4 to 6

carrot and sultana sambal

2 teaspoons vegetable oil

1 tablespoon black mustard seeds

½ cup (45g) shredded coconut

2 large carrots (360g), grated finely

½ cup (80g) sultanas

¼ cup (60ml) lemon juice

⅓ cup chopped fresh mint

Heat oil in small saucepan; cook seeds and coconut, stirring, until coconut just starts to brown. Combine the coconut mixture with remaining ingredients in medium bowl; mix well.

makes about 3 cups

tomato kasaundi

4 large tomatoes (1kg), chopped

1 medium onion (150g), chopped

4 cloves garlic, chopped

1 tablespoon sliced fresh ginger

4 small red chillies, chopped

2 teaspoons salt

2 teaspoons ground cumin

½ teaspoon ground turmeric

½ teaspoon chilli powder

¼ teaspoon ground cloves

2 tablespoons vegetable oil

¼ cup (60ml) white vinegar

⅓ cup (75g) sugar

Blend or process all ingredients until pureed. Transfer mixture to large saucepan; stir, without boiling, until sugar is dissolved. Bring to boil; immediately simmer, uncovered, 45 minutes, stirring occasionally, or until mixture is thickened slightly.

makes about 3 cups

coconut coriander chutney

1 tablespoon ghee

1 teaspoon black mustard seeds

2 teaspoons cumin seeds

1 teaspoon garam masala

2 curry leaves, torn

1½ cups (135g) shredded coconut

2 small green chillies, chopped

½ teaspoon salt

¼ cup fresh coriander leaves

1 clove garlic, crushed

½ cup (125ml) coconut milk

¼ cup (60ml) lime juice

Heat ghee in small frying pan; cook seeds and garam masala, stirring, until fragrant. Stir in curry leaves. Blend or process remaining ingredients until pureed; combine with spice mixture in medium bowl. Shape into a 12cm round on a serving plate.

serves 4 to 6

RELISHES

cucumber and mint raita

1 medium Lebanese cucumber (150g)
1 teaspoon ghee
¼ teaspoon cumin seeds
¼ teaspoon black mustard seeds
¼ teaspoon ground cumin
1 cup (250ml) yogurt
1 tablespoon lemon juice
1 clove garlic, crushed
¼ teaspoon cayenne pepper
1 tablespoon chopped fresh mint

Peel cucumber; halve lengthways, discard seeds. Chop cucumber coarsely. Heat ghee in small pan; cook seeds and cumin, stirring, until seeds pop; cool. Combine spice mixture with cucumber, yogurt, juice, garlic and pepper in small bowl. Cover; refrigerate at least 2 hours. Just before serving, gently stir in mint.
makes about 1¼ cups

date and tamarind chutney

75g dried tamarind
2 cups (500ml) boiling water
2 teaspoons vegetable oil
2 teaspoons black mustard seeds
2 teaspoons cumin seeds
500g fresh dates, seeded, chopped
¼ cup (60ml) malt vinegar

Combine tamarind and the boiling water in medium bowl; stand 30 minutes. Strain tamarind over bowl, pressing to extract all liquid; discard tamarind. Heat oil in small pan; cook seeds, stirring, until they pop. Combine dates with tamarind liquid, seeds and vinegar in medium pan. Simmer, uncovered, 5 minutes until mixture is almost dry. Blend or process until almost smooth. Spoon into hot sterilised jars, seal while hot.
makes about 2½ cups

spinach raita

500g spinach
1 tablespoon ghee
1 small onion (80g), chopped finely
½ teaspoon black mustard seeds
1 teaspoon cumin seeds
1 teaspoon ground cumin
¼ teaspoon chilli powder
2 teaspoons lemon juice
1 teaspoon salt
2 teaspoons chopped fresh mint
1⅓ cups (330ml) yogurt

Boil, steam or microwave spinach until just wilted; drain, cool. Squeeze excess liquid from spinach; shred spinach. Heat ghee in small pan; cook onion, stirring, until onion is browned lightly. Add seeds; cook, stirring, until seeds pop. Add remaining spices; cook, stirring, until fragrant. Add juice, remove from heat; cool. Combine salt, mint and yogurt in medium bowl; mix in spinach and onion mixture.
makes about 2 cups

lentils with garlic dressing

2 cups (400g) masoor dhal (red lentils), rinsed, drained

½ teaspoon ground ginger

1 teaspoon ground coriander

½ teaspoon sweet paprika

3½ cups (875ml) chicken stock

4 tablespoons ghee

2 teaspoons cumin seeds

2 medium onions (300g), sliced

8 cloves garlic, sliced finely

2cm piece ginger, sliced

1 long green chilli, sliced thinly

2 tablespoons shredded fresh mint

Combine dhal, ground spices and stock in a medium saucepan; simmer, uncovered, stirring occasionally, 30 minutes or until dhal is tender and mixture has thickened. Heat ghee in medium pan; cook cumin seeds, onions, garlic, ginger and chilli, stirring occasionally, until onions are brown. Stir mint leaves and half the onion mixture into lentils; top with remaining onion mixture.

makes about 4½ cups

tomato and eggplant pickle

1 large eggplant (500g)

1 tablespoon salt

2 tablespoons ghee

1 large onion (200g), chopped

3 cloves garlic, crushed

2 small red chillies, chopped

2 large tomatoes (500g), chopped

2 teaspoons sugar

1 teaspoon garam masala

1 teaspoon ground coriander

½ teaspoon chilli powder

1 tablespoon white vinegar

⅔ cup (160ml) water

Peel eggplant; cut into 1cm slices, sprinkle both sides with half the salt. Cover; stand 20 minutes. Rinse eggplant under cold water; pat dry, then chop eggplant into small pieces. Heat ghee in large pan; cook onion, garlic and chillies, stirring, until onion is browned lightly. Add eggplant; cook, stirring, 2 minutes. Add remaining salt, tomatoes, sugar, spices, vinegar and water; cook, stirring occasionally, about 15 minutes or until the mixture has thickened. Cool.

makes about 2½ cups

sweet mango chutney

2 tablespoons vegetable oil

1 tablespoon black mustard seeds

½ teaspoon cardamom seeds

1½ tablespoons cumin seeds

2 medium onions (300g), chopped

2 small red chillies, chopped

5 cloves garlic, crushed

1 tablespoon grated fresh ginger

1½ tablespoons ground coriander

3 teaspoons ground turmeric

6 medium mangoes (2.5kg), peeled, chopped

1 cup (170g) raisins, chopped

1⅓ cups (295g) caster sugar

2 teaspoons salt

1 cup (250ml) white wine vinegar

½ cup (125ml) malt vinegar

Heat oil in large heavy-based pan; cook seeds, stirring, until they pop. Add onions, chillies, garlic and ginger; cook, stirring, until onions are browned lightly. Add ground spices; cook, stirring, until mixture is fragrant. Add remaining ingredients; simmer, uncovered, about 1¼ hours, stirring occasionally, or until thickened. Pour the chutney into hot sterilised jars, seal while hot.

makes about 8 cups

RICE & BREAD

aromatic rice

1 Heat ghee in medium heavy-based saucepan; cook onions, garlic, spices and nuts, stirring, 5 minutes or until onions are browned lightly and mixture is fragrant.
2 Stir in rice and warm stock; simmer, covered, 15 minutes. Remove from heat; fluff with fork, then stand, covered, 10 minutes.

serves 4

1 tablespoon ghee

2 small onions (160g), sliced finely

3 cloves garlic, crushed

3 teaspoons cumin seeds

2 teaspoons black mustard seeds

4 cardamom pods, bruised

2 bay leaves

½ cup (75g) shelled pistachio nuts

1½ cups (300g) basmati rice, washed, drained

2¾ cups (680ml) warm chicken stock

Cook onions, garlic, spices and nuts until browned and fragrant.

Stir in rice and stock; simmer 15 minutes.

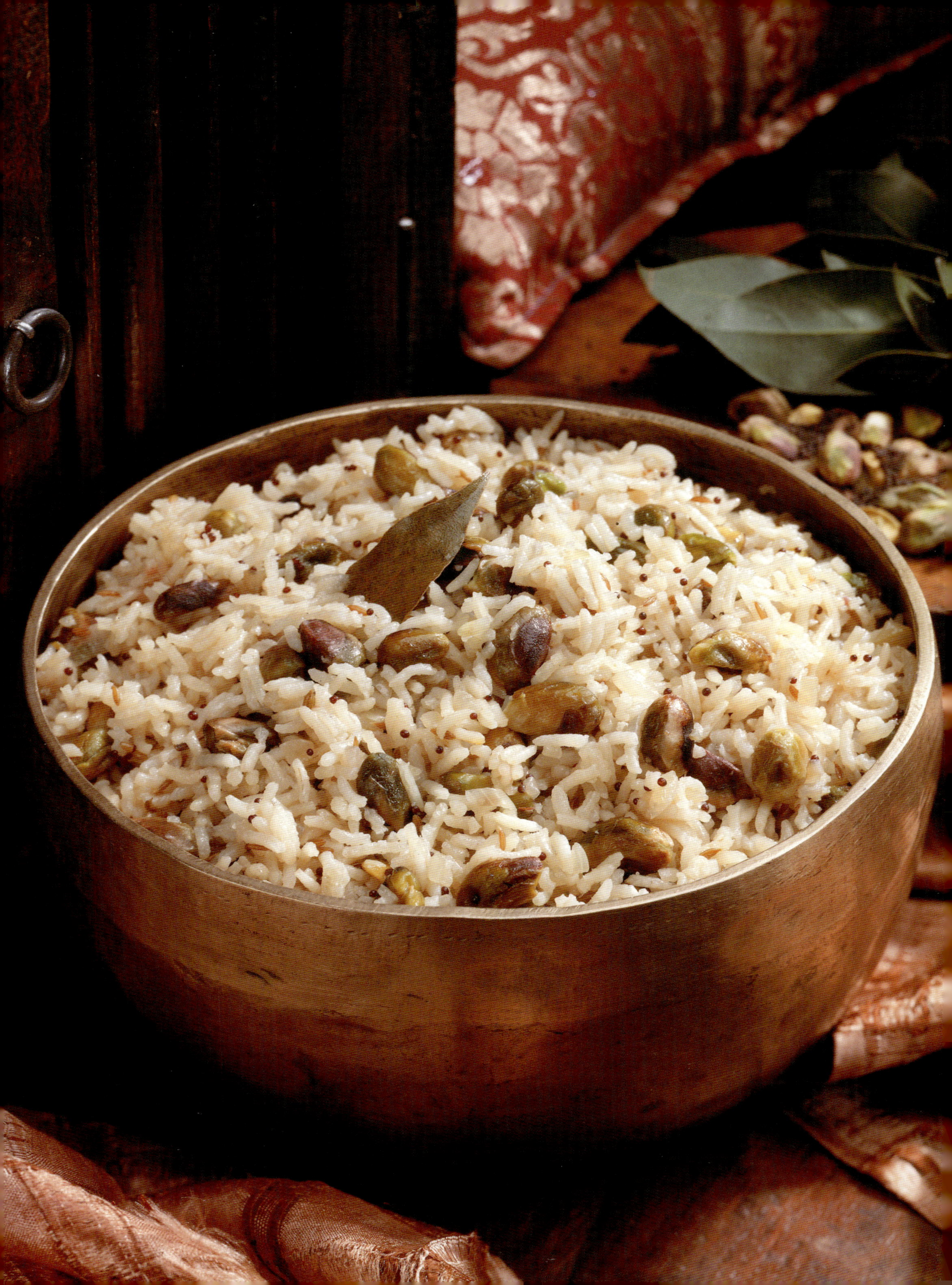

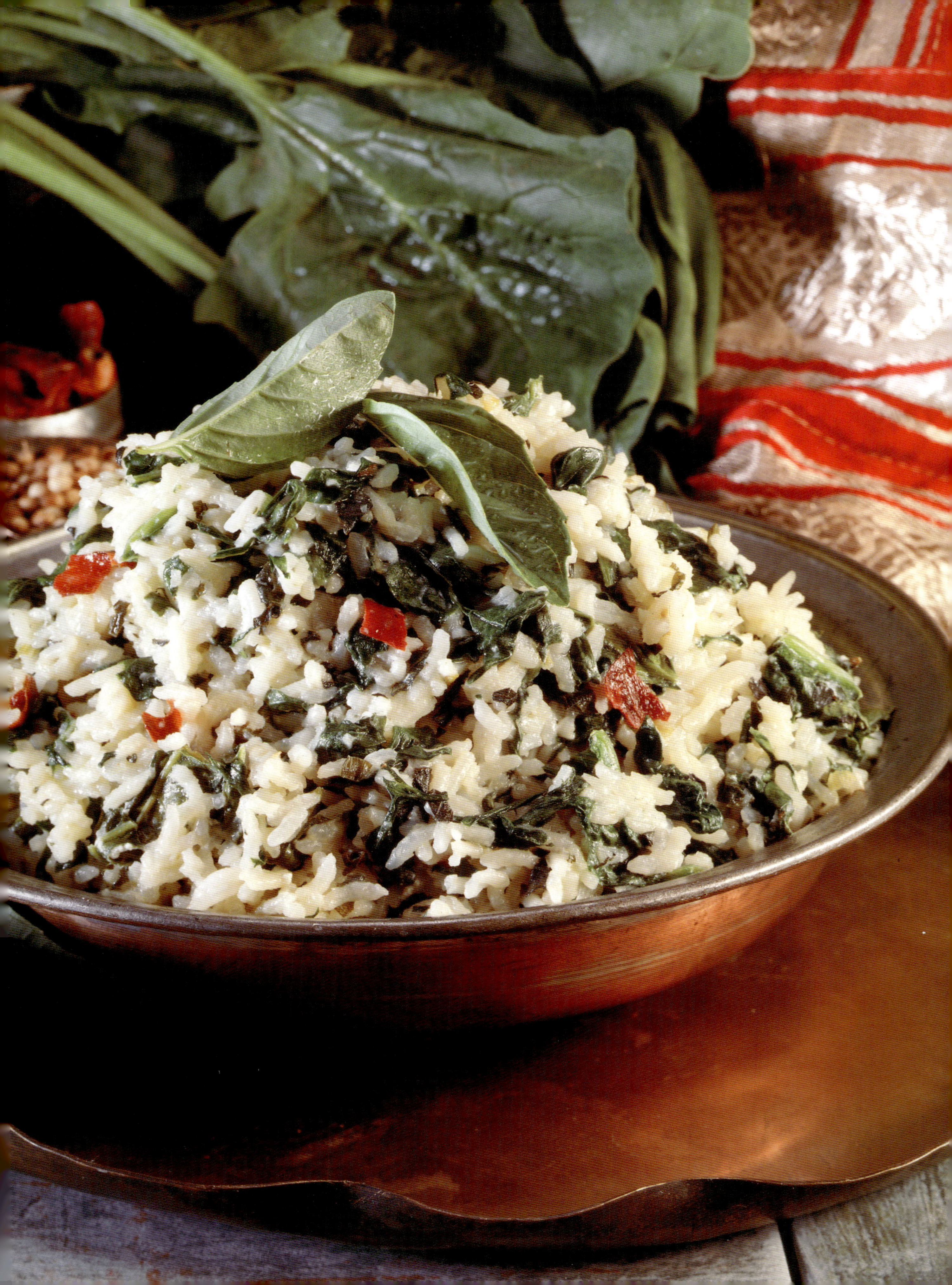

spinach pilau

2 tablespoons vegetable oil
6 green onions, sliced
2 dried red chillies, crushed
½ teaspoon coriander seeds
1 clove garlic, crushed
2 cups (400g) long-grain rice
1 litre (4 cups) water
1 tablespoon chicken stock powder
500g spinach, chopped
¼ cup chopped fresh basil
½ cup (125ml) yogurt

1 Heat vegetable oil in medium saucepan; cook onions, chillies, seeds and garlic, stirring, until fragrant.
2 Stir in rice; add water and stock powder. Boil; immediately simmer, covered, 15 minutes or until rice is tender and liquid absorbed.
3 Remove from heat; stir in spinach, basil and yogurt.

serves 4 to 6

Cook onions, chillies, seeds and garlic until fragrant.

Stir in rice, water and stock; simmer until rice is tender.

Remove from heat; stir in spinach, basil and yogurt.

lemon and saffron rice

1. Bring stock to boil in medium saucepan, remove from heat, stir in saffron; cover, stand 15 minutes.
2. Heat ghee in medium saucepan; cook onions, garlic, ginger and curry leaves, stirring, until onions are browned lightly. Stir in rind and rice.
3. Add stock to rice mixture; simmer, covered, 15 minutes or until rice is tender and liquid absorbed. Stir in juice and fresh coriander; stand, covered, 5 minutes.

serves 4 to 6

1 litre (4 cups) chicken stock
¼ teaspoon saffron threads
2 tablespoons ghee
2 small onions (160g), sliced
2 cloves garlic, crushed
1 teaspoon grated fresh ginger
6 curry leaves
2 teaspoons grated lemon rind
2 cups (400g) basmati rice, washed, drained
¼ cup (60ml) lemon juice
¼ cup chopped fresh coriander

Remove pan from heat, stir in saffron; stand 15 minutes.

Stir rind and rice into onion mixture, until coated.

Stir salt, rice and onions into spice mixture.

caramelised onion, fruit and nut pilau

2 tablespoons ghee

2 large onions (400g), sliced

2 tablespoons ghee, extra

1 teaspoon hot chilli powder

1 teaspoon ground black pepper

¼ teaspoon saffron threads

4 cardamom pods, bruised

4 cloves

1 cinnamon stick

1 teaspoon salt

2 cups (400g) basmati rice, washed, drained

1 litre (4 cups) water

½ cup (75g) currants

½ cup (75g) chopped dried apricots

½ cup (80g) sultanas

½ cup (70g) slivered almonds, toasted

1 Heat ghee in large saucepan; cook onions, stirring, 15 minutes or until caramelised. Remove from pan.
2 Add extra ghee and spices to same pan; cook, stirring until fragrant. Stir in salt, rice and onions.
3 Add water; boil, then immediately simmer, covered, 10 minutes or until rice is tender and water absorbed. Stir in currants, apricots and sultanas; stand, covered, 5 minutes. Just before serving, stir in nuts.

serves 4 to 6

Pour water into pan; simmer until rice is tender.

khitcherie

1. Place dhal in small bowl, cover with cold water; soak 1 hour. Drain well.
2. Heat ghee in medium saucepan; cook onion, garlic, chillies, ginger, spices, curry leaves and salt, stirring, until onion is browned lightly and mixture fragrant.
3. Add dhal, rice, raisins and water; boil, then immediately simmer, covered, 15 minutes or until rice is tender. Remove from heat, discard cinnamon, stir in juice; stand, covered, 5 minutes. Just before serving, stir in cashews.

serves 4 to 6

1 cup (200g) toor dhal (yellow split peas)

3 tablespoons ghee

1 medium onion (150g), chopped finely

2 cloves garlic, crushed

2 small green chillies, chopped finely

2 teaspoons finely grated fresh ginger

½ teaspoon ground turmeric

1 teaspoon cumin seeds

½ teaspoon garam masala

1 teaspoon ground coriander

1 cinnamon stick

4 curry leaves

2 teaspoons salt

1½ cups (300g) basmati rice, washed, drained

1 cup (170g) raisins

1 litre (4 cups) hot water

1 tablespoon lime juice

½ cup (75g) cashews, toasted

nawabi biryani

2 tablespoons ghee
2 medium onions (300g), sliced thinly
2 medium potatoes (400g), chopped
1 teaspoon cumin seeds
2 cups (400g) long-grain rice
1 litre (4 cups) water
1 cup (125g) frozen peas

MINT MASALA
½ cup firmly packed fresh mint leaves
2 long green chillies, chopped
2 tablespoons vegetable oil
½ teaspoon garam masala
1 teaspoon salt
¼ cup (35g) coconut milk powder
¼ cup (60ml) water

1 Heat ghee in large saucepan; cook onions and potatoes, stirring, until both are just browned lightly.
2 Blend or process all mint masala ingredients until pureed.
3 Add cumin seeds and mint masala to pan; cook, stirring, until fragrant. Stir in rice.
4 Add water to pan; simmer, covered, 10 minutes. Remove from heat, stir in peas; stand, covered, 10 minutes.

serves 4 to 6

Cook onions and potatoes until both are browned lightly.

Process mint masala ingredients until pureed.

RICE & BREAD

besani roti

1. Sift flours and salt into a medium bowl, rub in ghee; mix in enough water to make a firm dough. Knead dough on a floured surface 5 minutes or until smooth; cover, refrigerate 30 minutes.
2. Divide dough into 12 pieces; roll each piece, on a floured surface, into a 17cm round roti.
3. Brush roti on each side with extra ghee; cook, one at a time, on a heated tawa or dry non-stick frying pan, until brown on both sides. Keep roti warm while cooking remainder. Serve brushed with more melted ghee, if desired.

makes 12

1 cup (140g) besan (chickpea flour)

1 cup (160g) wholemeal plain flour

1 cup (140g) plain flour

1 teaspoon salt

3 tablespoons ghee

¾ cup (180ml) warm water, approximately

125g ghee, melted, extra, optional

Combine dry ingredients, ghee and enough water to make a firm dough.

Roll each piece of dough into a 17cm round roti.

Cook roti in non-stick frying pan until browned both sides.

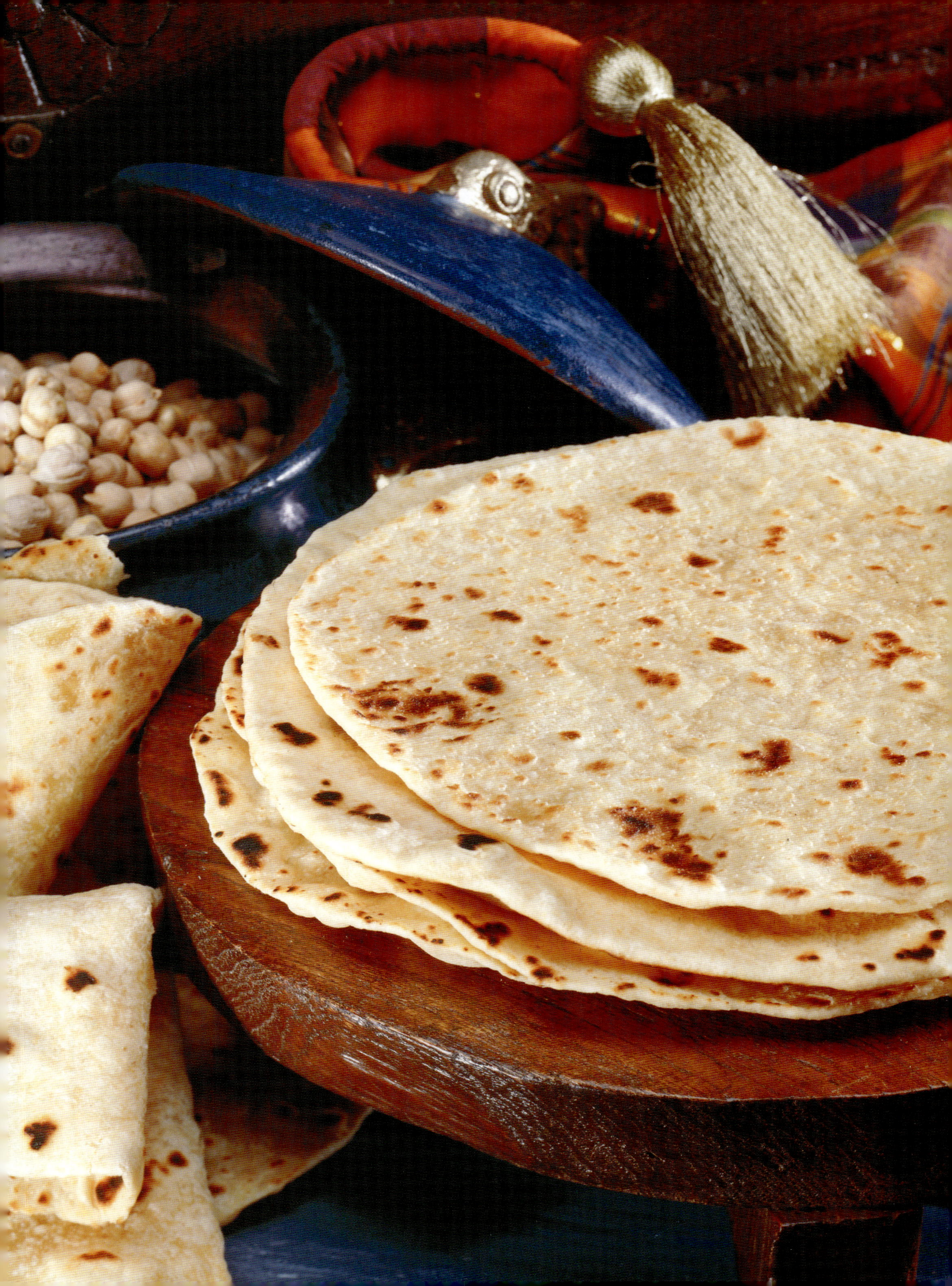

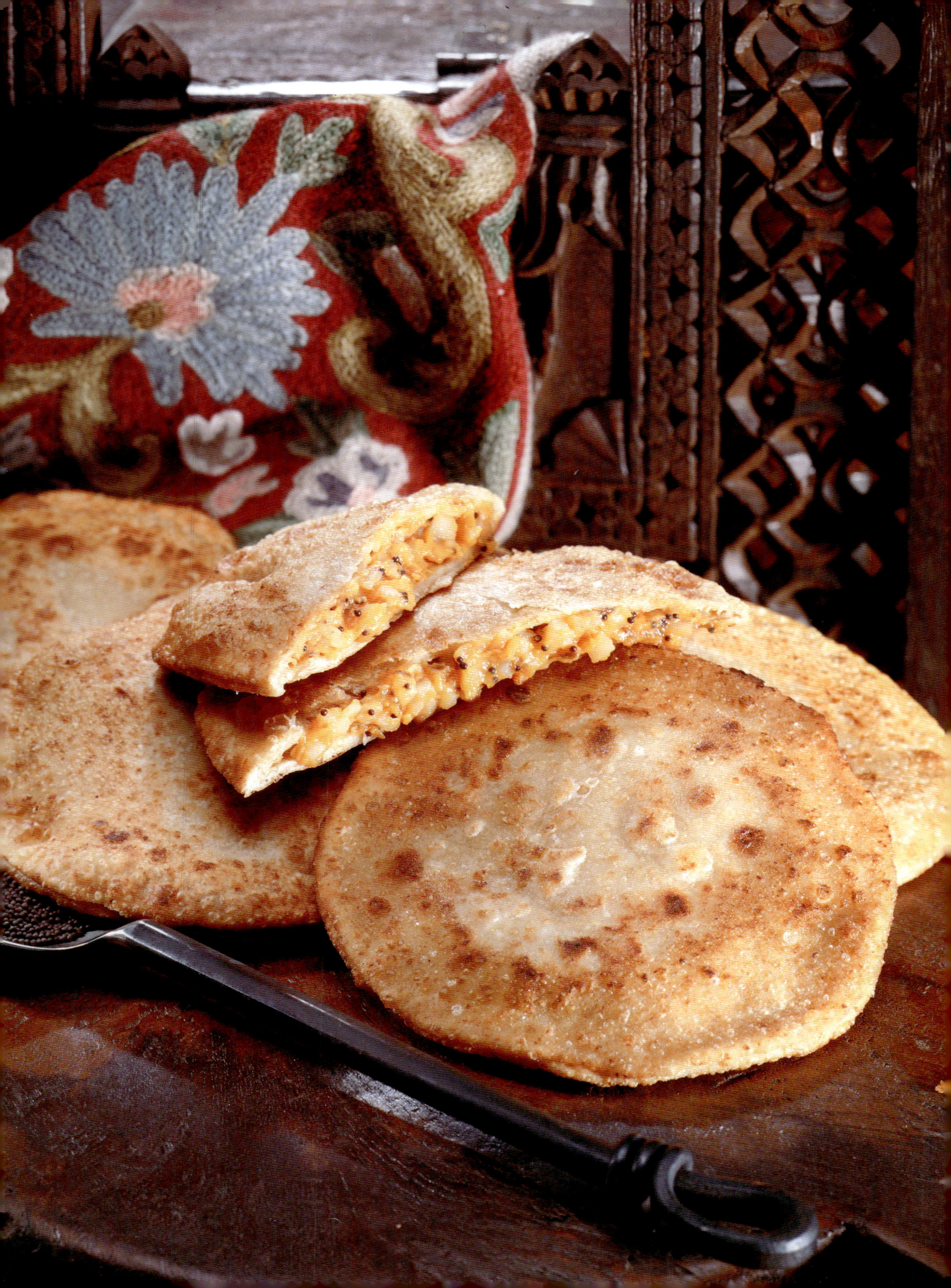

paratha with kumara and potato filling

1½ cups (240g) wholemeal plain flour
1½ cups (225g) plain flour
1 teaspoon salt
2 tablespoons ghee, melted
1 cup (250ml) water, approximately
¼ cup (60ml) vegetable oil

KUMARA AND POTATO FILLING
400g kumara, chopped
1 tablespoon vegetable oil
1 teaspoon salt
2 teaspoons cumin seeds
2 teaspoons black mustard seeds
2 small potatoes (240g), chopped finely
¾ cup (180ml) water

1. Process flours, salt, ghee and enough water until dough forms a ball. Knead dough on floured surface 10 minutes or until smooth and elastic; cover with plastic wrap, stand 1 hour.
2. Make kumara and potato filling.
3. Divide dough into 16 pieces; roll each piece, on a floured surface, into a 14cm round paratha. Layer paratha, separated by plastic wrap, into a stack.
4. Spread filling over eight paratha, leaving 1cm border on each; brush border with water. Top each with one of the remaining paratha, pressing edges together to seal.
5. Heat oil in large frying pan; cook filled paratha, one at a time, until browned on both sides. Drain on absorbent paper; keep warm while cooking remainder.

KUMARA AND POTATO FILLING Boil, steam or microwave the kumara until tender; drain, then mash. Heat oil in a medium saucepan; cook salt and seeds, stirring, until seeds pop. Add potatoes and water; cook, stirring, 10 minutes or until potatoes are just tender. Stir kumara into potato mixture; cool.

makes 8

Roll dough into 16 rounds; stack, separated with plastic wrap.

Spread filling over eight paratha, leaving 1cm border.

Cook filled paratha, one at a time, until brown both sides.

lentil and spinach chapati

1. Sift both flours and salt into large bowl; add oil and enough water to make a firm dough. Knead dough on a floured surface 10 minutes or until smooth and elastic; cover dough with plastic wrap, stand 1 hour.
2. Divide dough into 16 pieces; roll each piece, on a floured surface, into a 14cm round chapati. Layer all chapati, separated by plastic wrap, into a stack; cover with cloth.
3. Make lentil and spinach filling.
4. Spread filling over eight of the chapati, leaving a 1cm border on each; brush border with water. Top each with one of the remaining chapati, pressing edges together to seal.
5. Heat griddle or dry heavy-based frying pan; cook filled chapati, one at a time, until browned on both sides. Keep chapati warm while cooking remainder.

LENTIL AND SPINACH FILLING Heat oil in medium saucepan; cook onion and garlic, stirring, until onion is browned lightly. Add spices; cook, stirring, until fragrant. Add dhal and stock; simmer, uncovered, 20 minutes or until dhal is tender and all liquid absorbed. Add spinach; cool.

makes 8

1½ cups (225g) plain flour

½ cup (80g) wholemeal plain flour

1 teaspoon salt

1 tablespoon vegetable oil

¾ cup (180ml) warm water, approximately

LENTIL AND SPINACH FILLING

1 tablespoon vegetable oil

1 medium onion (150g), chopped

2 cloves garlic, crushed

1 teaspoon ground cumin

1 teaspoon garam masala

1½ teaspoons black mustard seeds

½ teaspoon ground turmeric

½ cup (100g) masoor dhal (red lentils), washed, drained

2 cups (500ml) chicken stock

250g spinach, shredded finely

Knead chapati dough until smooth and elastic.

Spread filling over half of the chapati, leaving 1cm border.

Cook filled chapati on griddle pan until brown both sides.

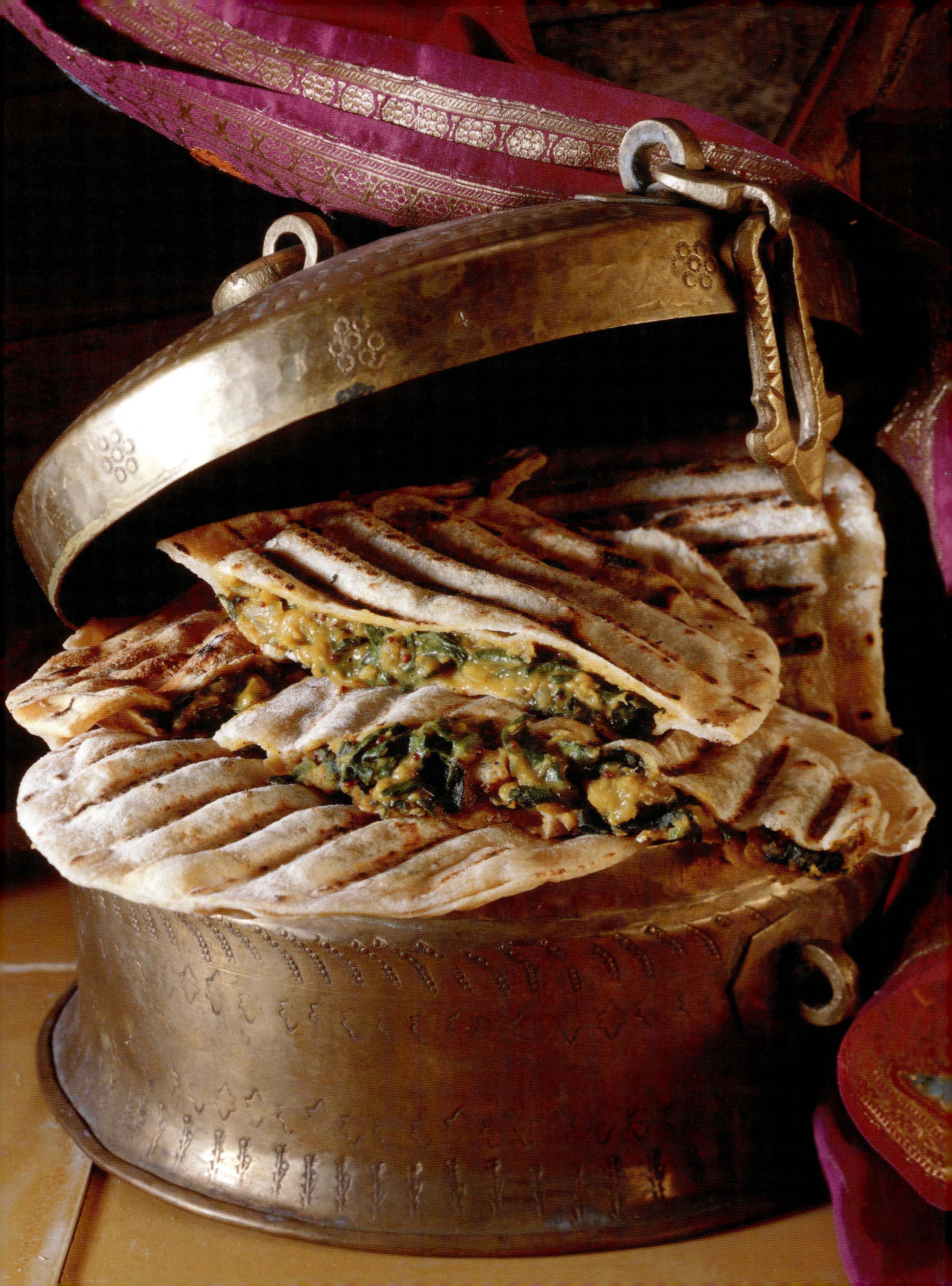

SWEETS & DRINKS

pistachio, saffron and cardamom kulfi

1. Combine milk, cream, cardamom pods and saffron in large heavy-based saucepan; boil, then immediately simmer, uncovered, 10 minutes or until reduced to 3 cups, stirring often. Add sugar, stir until dissolved.
2. Cool kulfi mixture, in pan, to room temperature. Strain into a large bowl; discard cardamom pods. Stir in nuts.
3. Divide the kulfi mixture among six ½-cup (125ml) moulds; cover with foil, freeze 3 hours or until firm. Just before serving, turn kulfi onto serving plates; accompany with fresh fruit or more toasted nuts, if desired.

serves 6

2 x 375g cans evaporated milk
¾ cup (180ml) cream
6 cardamom pods, bruised
¼ teaspoon crushed saffron threads
⅓ cup (75g) caster sugar
⅓ cup (50g) shelled pistachios, toasted, chopped finely

Simmer milk, cream, cardamom and saffron until reduced.

Strain kulfi mixture into large bowl; discard cardamom pods.

Freeze kulfi in moulds 3 hours or until firm.

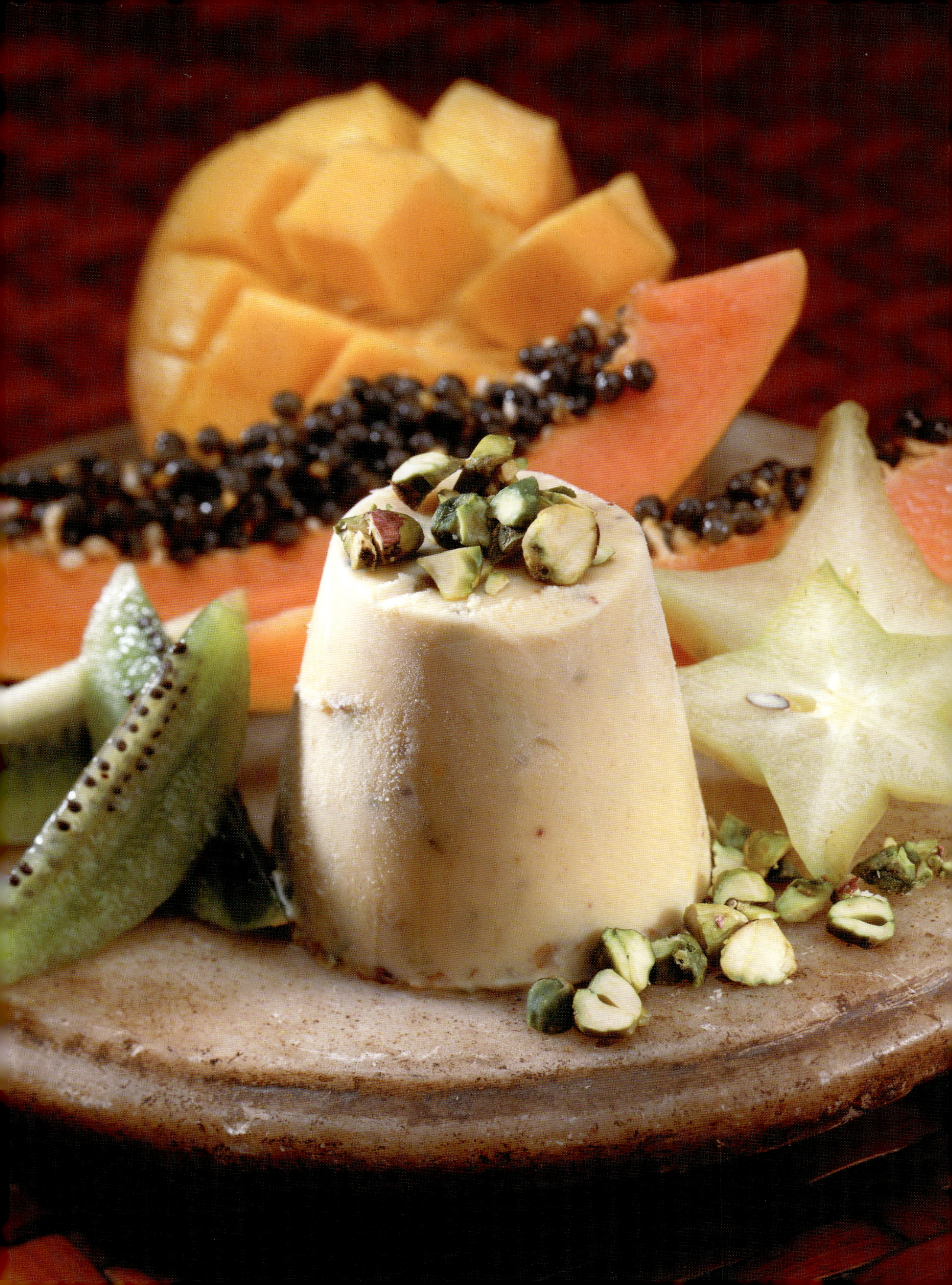

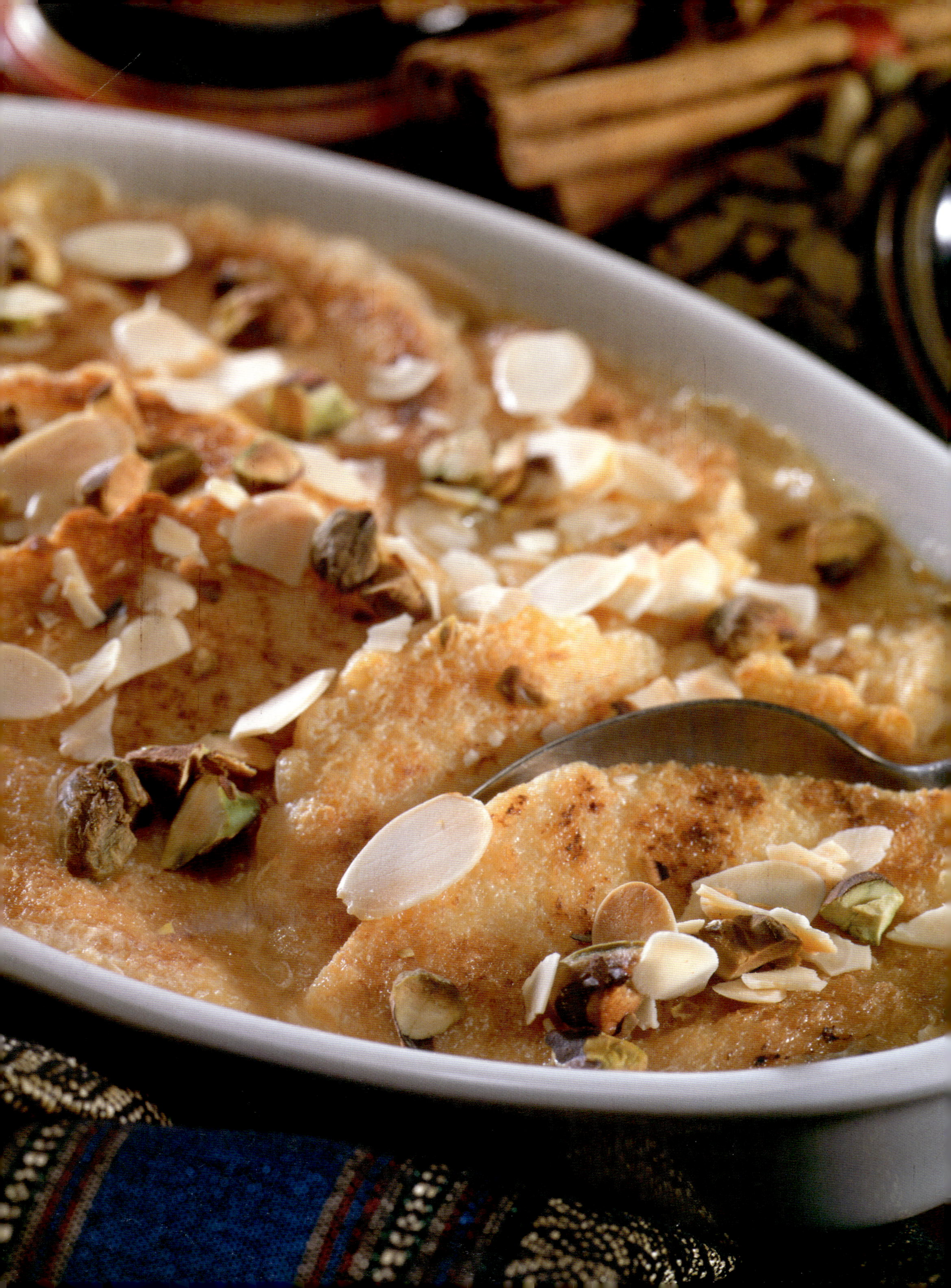

SWEETS & DRINKS

shahi turka

8 slices stale white bread
2 tablespoons ghee
375ml can evaporated milk
½ cup (125ml) milk
2 cinnamon sticks
6 cardamom pods, bruised
pinch saffron threads
¼ cup (55g) caster sugar
1 tablespoon flaked almonds
1 tablespoon chopped shelled pistachios

1. Preheat oven to moderate. Using a 9.5cm cutter, cut bread slices into rounds.
2. Heat half the ghee in a large frying pan; cook half the bread rounds until browned both sides. Repeat with remaining ghee and rounds.
3. Arrange rounds, overlapping slightly, in shallow 1-litre (4-cup) ovenproof dish.
4. Combine evaporated milk, milk, spices and sugar in large saucepan; stir over low heat until sugar is dissolved. Simmer, uncovered, 5 minutes, stirring occasionally. Strain milk mixture into a small bowl.
5. Pour milk mixture over bread rounds, sprinkle with nuts; stand 30 minutes. Bake, uncovered, in moderate oven 15 minutes or until browned lightly.

serves 4

Cut bread slices into rounds with a 9.5cm cutter.

Overlap bread rounds in shallow ovenproof dish.

Simmer milks, spices and sugar, stirring occasionally.

SWEETS & DRINKS

rose-flavoured milk custard

1. Bring milk to boil in medium saucepan; simmer, uncovered, 30 minutes or until reduced to 2 cups (500ml). Strain into a large bowl, then return to same pan.
2. Add condensed milk, rosewater, cardamom and enough food colouring to make milk mixture a pale custard colour. Simmer, uncovered, 15 minutes, stirring occasionally, or until thickened slightly.
3. Transfer custard to large bowl; stir in nuts. Cover; refrigerate 3 hours or overnight. Serve with fresh fruit, if desired.

serves 6 to 8

1 litre (4 cups) milk

400g can sweetened condensed milk

3 teaspoons rosewater

1 teaspoon ground cardamom

yellow food colouring

1 tablespoon chopped blanched almonds, toasted

2 teaspoons chopped shelled pistachios, toasted

Bring milk to boil; simmer until reduced to 2 cups.

Add remaining ingredients, except nuts; simmer until thickened.

Pour kulfi mixture into lamington pan; freeze.

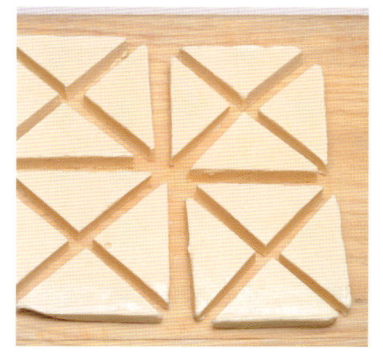

Cut kulfi into triangles on chopping board just before serving.

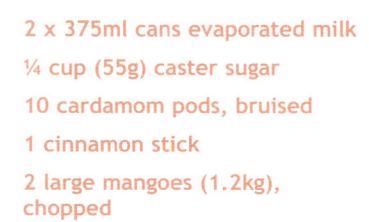

2 x 375ml cans evaporated milk
¼ cup (55g) caster sugar
10 cardamom pods, bruised
1 cinnamon stick
2 large mangoes (1.2kg), chopped

mango kulfi

1 Combine milk, sugar, cardamom and cinnamon in medium saucepan; boil then immediately simmer, 5 minutes. Stand 20 minutes; strain into bowl of food processor or blender. Discard spices.
2 Blend or process milk and mangoes until smooth. Pour kulfi mixture into lamington pan; cover with foil, freeze 1½ hours or until almost set.
3 Cover base and sides of 23cm-square slab pan with plastic wrap. Remove kulfi from freezer, roughly chop; blend or process until smooth. Pour into prepared pan; cover, freeze 3 hours or overnight.
4 Just before serving, turn kulfi onto chopping board; cut into 16 triangles.

serves 8

iced mango cooler

2 medium mangoes (860g)
36 ice cubes
1 tablespoon sugar

Halve mangoes, discard seeds; spoon mango flesh into the bowl of food processor or a blender. Process with ice cubes and sugar until thick and smooth. Pour into serving glasses; stand at room temperature for 5 minutes before serving.

makes about 3 cups

iced lime refresher

1 litre (4 cups) water
2/3 cup (150g) caster sugar
1/3 cup (80ml) lime juice
1 teaspoon shredded fresh mint
ice cubes

Combine water, sugar, juice and mint in large bowl; stir until sugar is dissolved. Cover, refrigerate 4 hours or until well chilled. Strain lime refresher into jug, serve poured over ice cubes.

makes about 5 cups

sweet saffron lassi

pinch saffron threads
1 tablespoon boiling water
2 cups (500ml) yogurt
1 cup (250ml) iced water
2 tablespoons caster sugar
½ teaspoon ground cardamom
ice cubes

Combine saffron and boiling water in small cup; stand 5 minutes. Whisk yogurt, iced water, sugar and cardamom in large jug; stir in saffron mixture. Serve lassi over ice cubes.

makes about 3 cups

masala chai

2 cinnamon sticks

1 teaspoon cardamom pods, bruised

1 teaspoon fennel seeds

½ teaspoon cloves

1 teaspoon ground ginger

½ teaspoon ground nutmeg

½ cup firmly packed fresh mint leaves

4 tea bags

2 cups (500ml) milk

2 cups (500ml) water

sugar, optional

Combine spices, mint and tea bags in teapot or heatproof jug. Bring combined milk and water to the boil, pour over spice mixture; stand 10 minutes. Sweeten with a little sugar, if desired. Just before serving, strain .

makes about 4 cups

1. Iced Mango Cooler
2. Iced Lime Refresher
3. Sweet Saffron Lassi
4. Masala Chai

SWEETS & DRINKS

kheer with fresh mango

1 Rinse rice until water runs clear. Place rice in a medium saucepan of boiling water; boil, uncovered, for 5 minutes. Drain well.
2 Bring milk, sugar, cardamom and cinnamon to the boil in a large saucepan. Immediately stir in the rice; simmer, uncovered, 20 minutes, stirring occasionally, or until most of the milk is absorbed. Remove from heat.
3 Stir in raisins, mangoes and half the almonds. Serve kheer drizzled with cream and sprinkled with remaining nuts.

serves 4

½ cup (100g) calrose rice
3 cups (750ml) milk
⅓ cup (75g) caster sugar
6 cardamom pods, bruised
¼ teaspoon ground cinnamon
¼ cup (40g) chopped raisins
3 large mangoes (1.8kg), chopped
⅓ cup (25g) flaked almonds, toasted
⅓ cup (80ml) cream

Drain partially cooked rice in strainer over bowl.

Stir raisins, mangoes and half the almonds into rice mixture.

Deep-fry balls in hot oil, in batches, until just browned.

Gently stir balls into hot syrup before serving.

gulab jamun

¾ cup (110g) plain flour
¼ cup (35g) self-raising flour
½ cup (60g) ground almonds
½ cup (50g) full cream milk powder
pinch ground cardamom
30g butter
¼ cup (60ml) yogurt
2 tablespoons water
vegetable oil, for deep-frying

SYRUP
3 cups (660g) caster sugar
5 cardamom pods, bruised
1 cup (250ml) water
¼ cup (35g) shelled pistachios
2 teaspoons rosewater

1 Sift flours, almonds, milk powder and cardamom into medium bowl; rub in butter. Stir in yogurt and water.
2 Roll heaped dessertspoons of the mixture into balls; deep-fry balls in hot oil, in batches, until just browned. Do not overheat the oil or balls will burn before they are cooked through. Drain on absorbent paper.
3 Make syrup.
4 Just before serving, stir balls gently into hot syrup.

SYRUP Mix sugar, cardamom and water in large saucepan; stir over heat, without boiling, until sugar is dissolved. Boil, uncovered, 5 minutes, without stirring, or until mixture is syrupy. Gently stir in nuts and rosewater.

makes about 30

basics

While important ingredients in authentic Indian cooking, these recipes will also serve you well when you make other ethnic food — the yogurt and cheese in Middle-Eastern cooking, the coconut milk and garma masala for Southeast Asian.

coconut milk

2 cups (180g) desiccated coconut
1 litre (4 cups) boiling water

Combine coconut and water in medium bowl; stand for 1 hour. Blend or process mixture until almost smooth. Squeeze mixture through fine muslin, extracting as much liquid as possible. Discard coconut.

makes about 3½ cups (875ml)

fresh cheese (paneer)

1 litre (4 cups) milk
2 tablespoons lemon juice
2 cups (500ml) cold water

Heat the milk in a large pan, stirring occasionally; boil then immediately simmer. Gradually stir in lemon juice until curds from; remove from heat, gently stir in water. Strain curds through muslin-lined strainer; rinse under cold running water untilthe liquid runs clear. Gather corners of muslin, tie together. Gently squeeze to extract as much moisture as possible, then hang muslin-wrapped cheese for about 1 hour. Press cheese under a heavy weight for about 1 hour or until cheese is firm; discard muslin.

makes about ½ cup (100g) cheese

garam masala

⅓ cup (20g) coriander seeds
2 tablespoons cumin seeds
2 teaspoons black peppercorns
2 teaspoons cardamom seeds
1 teaspoon cloves
1 teaspoon fennel seeds
1 cinnamon stick

Cook spices, one at a time, in heated dry frying pan until fragrant. Blend or process spices together until crushed.

makes about ⅓ cup

yogurt

3 cups (750ml) milk
2 tablespoons full cream milk powder
¼ cup (60ml) yogurt
2 teaspoon sugar

Whisk milk and powder in medium pan; whisk over heat until mixture comes to the boil, then immediately pour mixture into heatproof glass bowl, cover surface of mixture with plastic wrap. Cool to about 40°C or until the mixture is a little hotter than lukewarm. Stir in yogurt and sugar then pour mixture into heated vacuum flask; seal immediately. Otherwise, cover the bowl with plastic wrap then wrap in towels. Stand, undisturbed, at room temperature for about 24 hours. If flask was used, pour yogurt into medium bow; stir until smooth, then cover and refrigerate

makes about 2½ cups (625ml)

stocks

These stock recipes can be made up to 4 days ahead and stored, covered, in the refrigerator. Be sure to remove any fat from the surface after the cooled stock has been refrigerated overnight. If the stock is to be kept longer, it is best to freeze it in small quantities.

beef stock

2kg meaty beef bones
2 medium onions (300g)
2 trimmed celery stalks (200g), chopped
2 medium carrots (250g), chopped
3 bay leaves
2 teaspoons black peppercorns
5 litres (20 cups) water
3 litres (12 cups) water, extra

Place bones and unpeeled chopped onions in baking dish. Bake in hot oven 1 hour or until bones and onions are well browned. Transfer bones and onions to large saucepan; add celery, carrots, bay leaves, peppercorns and the water. Simmer, uncovered, 3 hours. Add the extra water; simmer, uncovered, further 1 hour. Strain.

makes about 2.5 litres (10 cups)

fish stock

1.5kg fish bones
3 litres (12 cups) water
1 medium onion (150g), chopped
2 trimmed celery stalks (200g), chopped
2 bay leaves
1 teaspoon black peppercorns

Combine all ingredients in large saucepan; simmer, uncovered, 20 minutes. Strain.

makes about 2.5 litres (10 cups)

chicken stock

2kg chicken bones
2 medium onions (300g), chopped
2 trimmed celery stalks (200g), chopped
2 medium carrots (250g), chopped
3 bay leaves
2 teaspoons black peppercorns
5 litres (20 cups) water

Combine all ingredients in large saucepan; simmer, uncovered, 2 hours. Strain.

makes about 2.5 litres (10 cups)

vegetable stock

2 large carrots (360g), chopped
2 large parsnips (360g), chopped
4 medium onions (600g), chopped
12 trimmed celery sticks (1.2kg), chopped
4 bay leaves
2 teaspoons black peppercorns
6 litres (24 cups) water

Combine all ingredients in large saucepan; simmer, uncovered, 1½ hours. Strain.

makes about 2.5 litres (10 cups)

glossary

ALMONDS

ground we used packaged commercially ground nuts.

slivered nuts that have been cut lengthways.

ASAFOETIDA resin from an onion-like bulb, sold in gum or powdered form. Used as a seasoning, in minute quantities, to substitute for garlic or onion; best known for its anti-flatulent properties, thus its inclusion in dhal.

BANANA LEAVES order from greengrocers. One leaf cuts into 10 pieces that are a suitable size for wrapping and steaming individual portions. Cut with sharp knife towards centre stem; immerse briefly in hot water to make leaves pliable.

BAY LEAVES leaves from the bay laurel tree; used fresh or dried.

BEEF

chuck steak from neck.

minced ground.

BESAN see FLOUR, chickpea.

BRUISE a cooking technique where the flat side of a chef's knife is pressed firmly down on certain herbs or spices, such as lemon grass or cardamom, to release the aroma or taste.

BUTTER use salted or unsalted (sweet) butter; 125g is equal to one stick of butter.

BUTTERMILK made by adding a culture to low-fat milk to give a slightly acidic flavour; a low-fat milk can be substituted, if preferred.

CAPSICUM also known as peppers or sweet peppers.

CARDAMOM native to India and used extensively in its cooking; can be purchased in pod, seed or ground form. Has an aromatic, distinctive, sweetly rich taste, and is one of the world's most expensive spices.

CHEESE

paneer a simple, delicate fresh cheese used as a major source of protein in the Indian diet; substitute it with ricotta.

ricotta fresh, unripened light curd cheese.

CHICKPEAS also known as garbanzos or channa; an irregularly round, sandy-coloured legume used extensively in Mediterranean and Indian cooking. Can be purchased canned, dried or roasted.

CHILLI available in many different types and sizes. Use rubber gloves when chopping fresh chillies as they can burn your skin. Removing seeds and membranes decreases the heat level.

powder the Asian variety is the hottest, made from ground chillies; it can be used as a substitute for fresh chillies in proportions of ½ teaspoon chilli powder to 1 medium chopped fresh chilli.

COCONUT

cream available in cans and cartons; made from coconut and water.

desiccated unsweetened concentrated, dried shredded coconut.

freshly grated can be grated from whole fresh coconut or purchased, frozen, in packets.

milk pure, unsweetened coconut milk available in cans.

milk powder coconut milk that has been dehydrated and ground to a fine powder.

COLOURINGS we used concentrated liquid vegetable food colourings.

CORIANDER also known as dhania, cilantro or chinese parsley; bright-green leafed herb with a pungent flavour. Also available ground and in seed form; roots and stems can also be used. Fresh leaves are often stirred into a completed curry just before serving to add a special aroma.

CREAM fresh pouring cream, minimum fat content of 35%; in Indian cooking, this is used in preference to cream that has been thickened commercially.

CURRY LEAVES bright-green, shiny, sharp-ended leaves having a flavour similar to traditional curry powders, hence their name; are used fresh or dried.

DATE AND TAMARIND CHUTNEY can be purchased ready-made in Indian specialty shops and some supermarkets. To make your own fresh chutney, see the recipe on page 88.

DHAL legumes such as lentils, dried peas and beans.

channa also known as chickpeas or garbanzos; see CHICKPEAS.

masoor also known as red lentils.

moong also known as split mung beans, these are the same pale-yellow pulse used to make bean sprouts.

toor also known as toovar or arhar dhal; an ochre-coloured split pea.

EGGPLANT also known as aubergine or brinjal.

FENUGREEK hard, dried seed usually sold ground as an astringent spice powder. Good with seafood and in chutneys. Fenugreek helps mask unpleasant odours.

FLOUR

chickpea made from ground chickpeas; also known as garam flour or besan.

plain all-purpose flour.

wholemeal plain wholewheat flour without the addition of baking powder.

GARAM MASALA a combination of powdered spices, consisting of cardamom, cinnamon, cloves, coriander, cumin and nutmeg in varying proportions. Sometimes black pepper is used to make a hot variation.

GHEE a pure butter fat available in cans; can be heated to high temperatures without burning due to its lack of salt and milk solids.

GINGER

fresh, green or root scrape away skin and grate, chop or slice as required.

ground should not be substituted for fresh ginger in any recipe.

GREEN ONIONS also called scallions, eschalots and green shallots. Do not confuse with the small golden shallots.

HERBS we have specified when to use fresh or dried herbs. Use dried (not ground) herbs in the proportion of 1:4 for fresh herbs, eg. 1 teaspoon dried herbs instead of 4 teaspoons (1 tablespoon) chopped fresh herbs.

JAGGERY also known as gur; a moulded lump sugar made from either distilled sugarcane or palm juice. Available from Asian specialty shops; substitute dark brown sugar.

KALONJI also known as black onion seeds or nigella.

KUMARA also known as orange-fleshed sweet potato.

LAMB

cutlet small tender rib chop.

diced cubed lean meat.

french-trimmed shanks also known as drumsticks or frenched shanks; all the gristle and the narrow end of the bone is discarded then the remaining meat trimmed.

leg cut from hindquarter.

minced ground lamb.

LEBANESE CUCUMBER long, slender and thin-skinned; this variety also known as the european or burpless cucumber.

LENTILS dried pulses. There are many different varieties of lentils, usually identified and named after their colour, such as red, brown and yellow (split peas).

MASALA literally meaning blended spices; a masala can be whole spices, a paste or powder, and can include herbs as well as spices and other seasonings. Traditional dishes are usually based on and named after particular masalas.

MILK we used full cream homogenised milk unless otherwise specified.

evaporated unsweetened canned milk, from which water has been extracted by evaporation.

full cream powder instant powdered milk from whole cow milk with all liquid removed and emulsifiers added.

sweetened condensed milk we used canned milk where 60% of the water has been removed; the remaining milk is sweetened with sugar.

MUSTARD SEEDS can be black or yellow.

OIL

corn an odourless, bland oil, obtained from corn kernels; has a high smoke point.

peanut pressed from ground peanuts; used frequently in stir-frying because of its high smoke point.

sesame made from roasted, crushed white sesame seeds; used as a flavouring rather than a cooking medium.

vegetable any of a wide number of oils having a plant, rather than an animal, source. We used a polyunsaturated vegetable oil.

OKRA a green, ridged, immature seed pod, also known as lady's fingers.

PANCH PHORA a combination of five aromatic seeds — mustard, fennel, cumin, fenugreek and kalonji (black onion) — fried in hot oil before use in various dishes.

PAPPADUMS sun-dried wafers made from a combination of lentil and rice flours, oil and spices; shallow- or deep-fry, or microwave, to reconstitute. Eaten on their own as a snack, with pickles and chutneys, or crumbled.

PAPRIKA ground dried peppers; sweet or hot.

PRAWNS also known as shrimp.

PUMPKIN we used various types, however one can be substituted for the other.

RIND also known as zest.

ROSEWATER extract made from crushed rose petals, called gulab in India; used for its aromatic quality in many sweetmeats and desserts.

SAAG the Indian name for spinach; also known as palak.

SAFFRON stigma of a member of crocus family, available in strands or ground form; imparts a yellow-orange colour to food once infused. Quality varies greatly; the best is the most expensive spice in the world. Store in freezer.

SNAKE BEANS long (about 40cm), thin, round green beans, similar in taste to string beans and runner beans.

SPINACH true spinach (the green vegetable often called spinach is correctly known as silverbeet) with delicate, crinkled green leaves on thin stems. High in iron, it's best cooked only until it has wilted.

STAR ANISE the dried star-shaped pod of an evergreen tree, it has an aniseed flavour.

STOCK 1 cup (250ml) stock is the equivalent of 1 cup (250ml) water plus 1 crumbled stock cube (or 1 teaspoon stock powder). Make your own fresh stock (see basics), if you prefer.

SUGAR we used coarse granulated table sugar, also known as crystal sugar, unless otherwise specified.

brown a soft, fine granulated sugar containing molasses, which provides its characteristic colour.

caster also known as superfine; fine granulated table sugar.

icing also known as confectioners' sugar or powdered sugar.

SWEET POTATO fleshy white root vegetable.

TANDOORI POWDER a flavourless mixture of yellow- and red-coloured powdered vegetable dyes, available from Indian food stores. Substitute normal red food colouring if desired, not turmeric.

TOMATO

paste a concentrated puree used in flavouring soups, stews, sauces and casseroles, etc.

puree canned pureed tomatoes (not tomato paste). Use fresh, peeled, pureed tomatoes as a substitute, if desired.

VANILLA BEAN dried bean of vanilla orchid. It can be used repeatedly; wash in warm water after use, dry well and store in airtight container.

YEAST allow 2 teaspoons (7g) dried yeast to each 15g compressed yeast if substituting one for other.

ZUCCHINI also known as courgette.

index

aloo tikka 16
aromatic rice 90

bandami lamb 58
beef
  biryani 85
  dhansak 65
  kofta with eggplant and tomato masala 69
  madras 82
besani roti 98
bombay mix 6
brinjal mollee 29
butter chicken 44

caramelised onion, fruit and nut pilau 95
cauliflower, pea and potato bhaji 21
channa dhal 28
cheese kofta in creamy tomato sauce 22
chicken
  butter 44
  chettinad 51
  dry, curry 50
  ishtew 53
  masala, drumsticks 46
  red, curry 49
  south indian, curry 45
  tikka 42
  with lentils and spinach 48
crunchy potatoes bengali-style 12
curry
  dry chicken 50
  goan fish 37
  mixed vegetable 26
  pork and tamarind 81
  prawn and green mango 39
  red chicken 49
  south indian chicken 45
  spinach and pumpkin 24

dhal
  and spinach soup 8
  channa, 28
  mixed, 27
drinks
  iced lime refresher 110
  iced mango cooler 110
  masala chai 111
  sweet saffron lassi 110
dry chicken curry 50

fish kofta 33
fish makhanwala 38

goan fish curry 37
gulab jamun 113

kashmiri lamb kofta 61
kheer with fresh mango 112
khitcherie 96
kofta
  beef, with eggplant and tomato masala 69
  cheese, in creamy tomato sauce 22
  fish 33
  kashmiri lamb 61
kumara and potato filling, paratha with 101

lamb
  bandami 58
  do piaza 66
  kashmiri, kofta 61
  kheema 77
  korma 70
  moglai leg of 78
  punjabi, shanks in spinach and tomatoes 62
  raan 73
  rogan josh 57
  tandoori, cutlets 54

lemon and saffron rice 94
lentil and spinach chapati 102

mango kulfi 109
masala chicken drumsticks 46
meat and vegetable samosas 11
mixed dhal 27
mixed vegetable curry 26
moglai leg of lamb 78
mulligatawny soup 15
mussel masala 41

nawabi biryani 97

paratha with kumara and potato filling 101
pilau, caramelised onion, fruit and nut 95
pilau, spinach 93
pistachio, saffron and cardamon kulfi 104
pork
  and tamarind curry 81
  vindaloo 74
prawn and green mango curry 39
prawn patia 34
prawns dhania masala 30
pumpkin curry, spinach and 24
punjabi lamb shanks in spinach and tomatoes 62

raan 73
red chicken curry 49
relishes
  banana and coconut sambal 86
  carrot and sultana sambal 87
  coconut coriander chutney 87
  cucumber and mint raita 88
  date and tamarind chutney 88
  lentils with garlic dressing 89
  spinach raita 88
  sweet mango chutney 89
  tomato and eggplant pickle 89
  tomato and mint kachumber 86
  tomato kasaundi 87
rogan josh 57
rose-flavoured milk custard 108

shahi turka 107
south indian chicken curry 45
spiced snake beans 20
spicy mixed nuts 7
spicy okra 25
spinach
  and pumpkin curry 24
  chicken with lentils and, 48
  dhal and, soup 89
  lentil and, chapati 102
  pilau 93

tandoori lamb cutlets 54
tikka
  aloo 16
  chicken 42

vegetable and lentil sambar 18
vegetable pakoras 4

conversion chart

Wherever you live, you'll be able to use our recipes with the help of these easy-to-follow conversions. While these conversions are approximate only, the difference between an exact and the approximate conversion of various liquid and dry measures is minimal and will not affect your cooking results.

LIQUID MEASURES

METRIC	IMPERIAL
30ml	1 fluid oz
60ml	2 fluid oz
100ml	3 fluid oz
125ml	4 fluid oz
150ml	5 fluid oz (¼ pint/1 gill)
190ml	6 fluid oz
250ml	8 fluid oz
300ml	10 fluid oz (½ pint)
500ml	16 fluid oz
600ml	20 fluid oz (1 pint)
1000ml (1 litre)	1¾ pints

MEASURING EQUIPMENT

The difference between one country's measuring cups and another's is, at most, within a 2 or 3 teaspoon variance. (For the record, one Australian metric measuring cup holds approximately 250ml.) The most accurate way of measuring dry ingredients is to weigh them. When measuring liquids, use a clear glass or plastic jug with the metric markings. (One Australian metric tablespoon holds 20ml; one Australian metric teaspoon holds 5ml.)

DRY MEASURES

METRIC	IMPERIAL
15g	½oz
30g	1oz
60g	2oz
90g	3oz
125g	4oz (¼lb)
155g	5oz
185g	6oz
220g	7oz
250g	8oz (½lb)
280g	9oz
315g	10oz
345g	11oz
375g	12oz (¾lb)
410g	13oz
440g	14oz
470g	15oz
500g	16oz (1lb)
750g	24oz (1½lb)
1kg	32oz (2lb)

LENGTH MEASURES

METRIC	IMPERIAL
3mm	⅛in
6mm	¼in
1cm	½in
2cm	¾in
2.5cm	1in
5cm	2in
6cm	2½in
8cm	3in
10cm	4in
13cm	5in
15cm	6in
18cm	7in
20cm	8in
23cm	9in
25cm	10in
28cm	11in
30cm	12in (1ft)

HOW TO MEASURE

When using graduated metric measuring cups, shake dry ingredients loosely into the appropriate cup. Do not tap the cup on a bench or tightly pack the ingredients unless directed to do so. Level top of measuring cups and measuring spoons with a knife. When measuring liquids, place a clear glass or plastic jug with metric markings on a flat surface to check accuracy at eye level.

Note: North America, NZ and the UK use 15ml tablespoons. All cup and spoon measurements are level.

We use large eggs having an average weight of 60g.

OVEN TEMPERATURES

These oven temperatures are only a guide for conventional ovens. For fan-forced ovens, check the manufacturer's manual.

	°C (CELSIUS)	°F (FAHRENHEIT)	GAS MARK
Very slow	120	250	½
Slow	150	275-300	1-2
Moderately slow	170	325	3
Moderate	180	350-375	4-5
Moderately hot	200	400	6
Hot	220	425-450	7-8
Very hot	240	475	9

This edition published in 2012 by Octopus Publishing Group Limited
based on materials licensed to it by ACP Magazines Ltd,
a division of PBL Media Pty Limited
54 Park St, Sydney
GPO Box 4088, Sydney, NSW 2001.
phone (02) 9282 8618; fax (02) 9267 9438
acpbooks@acpmagazines.com.au; www.acpbooks.com.au

acp books

ACP BOOKS
General Manager - Christine Whiston
Editor-in-Chief - Susan Tomnay
Creative Director - Hieu Chi Nguyen
Food Director - Pamela Clark

OCTOPUS BOOKS
Published and Distributed in the United Kingdom by
Octopus Publishing Group Limited
Endeavour House
189 Shaftesbury Avenue
London WC2H 8JY
United Kingdom
phone (+44)(0)207 632 5400; fax (+44)(0)207 632 5405
aww@octopusbooks.co.uk; www.octopusbooks.co.uk;
www.australian-womens-weekly.com

Printed and bound in China

International foreign language rights, Brian Cearnes, ACP Books bcearnes@acpmagazines.com.au

A catalogue record for this book is available from the British Library.
ISBN 978-1-907428-64-7
© ACP Magazines Ltd 2010
ABN 18 053 273 546

This publication is copyright. No part of it may be reproduced or transmitted
in any form without the written permission of the Publisher.

This book was originally published in 1997. Reprinted 1999, 2000, 2001, 2002, 2004.
Revised and updated 2005, reprinted 2005.

To order Australian Women's Weekly Books:
telephone LBS on 01903 828 503
or order online at www.australian-womens-weekly.com
or www.octopusbooks.co.uk